Up the Creek
A Paddler's Guide to Ontario

Up the Creek

A Paddler's Guide to Ontario

Kevin Callan

The BOSTON
MILLS PRESS

CATALOGUING IN PUBLICATION
DATA

Callan, Kevin
Up the creek : a paddler's guide to Ontario

Includes bibliographical references.
ISBN 1-55046-167-2

1. Canoes and canoeing – Ontario –
Guidebooks.
2. Ontario – Guidebooks. I. Title

GV776.15.05C35 1996   797.1'22'09713
C96-930274-6

Copyright ©1996 Kevin Callan

Reprinted in 2000 by
BOSTON MILLS PRESS
132 Main Street
Erin, Ontario N0B 1T0
Tel 519-833-2407
Fax 519-833-2195
e-mail books@bostonmillspress.com
www.bostonmillspress.com

An affiliate of
STODDART PUBLISHING CO. LIMITED
34 Lesmill Road
Toronto, Ontario, Canada
M3B 2T6
Tel 416-445-3333
Fax 416-445-5967
e-mail gdsinc@genpub.com

Distributed in Canada by
GENERAL DISTRIBUTION SERVICES LIMITED
325 Humber College Boulevard
Toronto, Canada M9W 7C3
Orders 1-800-387-0141 Ontario & Quebec
Orders 1-800-387-0172 NW Ontario
& other provinces
e-mail cservice@genpub.com

Distributed in the United States by
GENERAL DISTRIBUTION SERVICES INC.
PMB 128, 4500 Witmer Industrial Estates,
Niagara Falls, New York 14305-1386
Toll-free 1-800-805-1083
Toll-free fax 1-800-481-6207
e-mail gdsinc@genpub.com
www.genpub.com

Photographs by the author
Design by Mary Firth
Printed in Canada

THE CANADA COUNCIL | LE CONSEIL DES ARTS
FOR THE ARTS | DU CANADA
SINCE 1957 | DEPUIS 1957

We acknowledge for their financial support of our
publishing program the Canada Council, the
Ontario Arts Council, and the Government of Canada
through the Book Publishing Industry
Development Program (BPIDP).

Contents

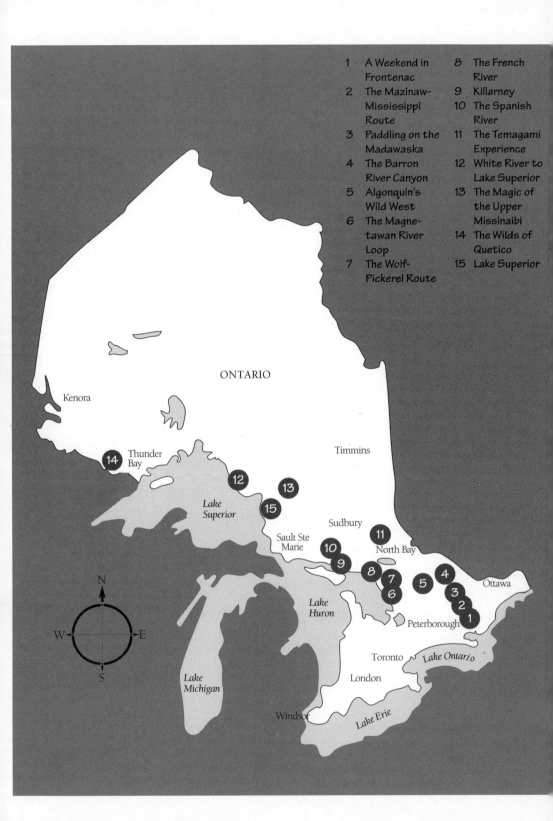

ONTARIO

Kenora

Timmins

Thunder Bay

Lake Superior

Sudbury

Sault Ste Marie

North Bay

Ottawa

Lake Huron

Peterborough

N

W — E

S

Toronto

Lake Ontario

Lake Michigan

London

Windsor

Lake Erie

Preface

If Canadian film producers ever wanted to depict the opening up of Ontario's wilderness the way Hollywood characterized winning the Wild West, the hero wouldn't be straddling a horse, but rather crouched down in a canoe, paddling off into the sunset. After all, the packsack, paddle and portage are as much pioneer icons as the chuckwagon, boot spur and ten-gallon hat. Maybe the closest this aspect of Canadian culture has come to be represented in film (the work of the late Bill Mason excluded) is with the Frantics' Mr. Canoehead, a superhero who had his head inadvertently welded to his aluminum canoe by a stray lightning bolt.

Nonetheless, on screen or off, Canadian identity lies with the canoe. When I spot a car barrelling down Highway 401 with a canoe strapped to its roof, I don't necessarily see a somewhat inexpensive recreational watercraft owned by some poor fool who can't afford a speedboat; I see a way of life.

Up the Creek is all about that way of life. This book guides whitewater fanatics down rushing rivers, seasoned trippers across remote lakes, and first-time family canoeists on perfect weekend outings.

Writing this book would have been impossible without the help of many people. I would first like to thank all my paddling companions who have tagged along for the field work for this book: Scott Roberts, Mike Walker, Doug Galloway, Peter Fraser, Brian Reid, John Glasgow, John Buck, Neil Steffler, Al McPherson, Heather Hall, Anne Swarbrick, Pat and Paul Lillies, Dave, Karen and Sarah Hicks, and especially my wife, Alana.

Special thanks also to all the Ministry of Natural Resources staff and the outfitters who helped organize my trips ... except maybe the park employee who shuttled my truck to the take-out on the White River and forgot to turn my lights off!

As well, I want to thank Hiker's Haven for being behind me since day one, Mike Cullen and staff at Trent Photographics for their expertise, the gang at Wild Rock Outfitters for showing great interest in the development of this book, and John Denison and Noel Hudson of Boston Mills Press for being the only publisher and editor in the business who would come to my wedding dressed in furry beaver costumes.

And finally, I would like to thank my parents for all their support and for only occasionally questioning my strange desire to become a full-time Canoehead.

Baby Sarah was a priceless addition to our weekend in Frontenac.

1 A Weekend in Frontenac

Unlike many canoeists who simply give up canoe tripping when they have children, our friends Dave and Karen Hicks looked upon their baby, Sarah, as a priceless addition to their canoeing getaways rather than a reason to keep out of the woods.

Curious about what it would be like to canoe with kids, but not eager enough to bear our own child, Alana and I took the easy way out and tagged along with the Hicks family on a weekend excursion to Frontenac Provincial Park's Big Salmon Lake.

After turning off Highway 38 onto Perth Road, north of Kingston, and picking up our vehicle permit at the park office trail centre (booking a reservation for this route is strongly recommended), we drove down bumpy Salmon Road to the designated launch site. Alana and I unlashed the canoe from the truck racks, carried it down to the dock, tossed in our gear, and then sat adrift for twenty minutes as we waited for Dave and Karen to find room in their canoe for the seemingly endless baby paraphernalia. It quickly became obvious why we had chosen a route free of any portages. In fact, it soon became evident that this trip would be entirely free of many things usually associated with a regular canoe trip.

We made base camp halfway along Big Salmon Lake, at one of the three cluster sites (all campsites are made up of two to four sites, with a limit of six persons and two small tents per site), and making use of the maze of portages and hiking trails that interconnect throughout the park's interior, we shouldered our daypacks and explored Frontenac's historical treasures.

"Let's go, Dad."

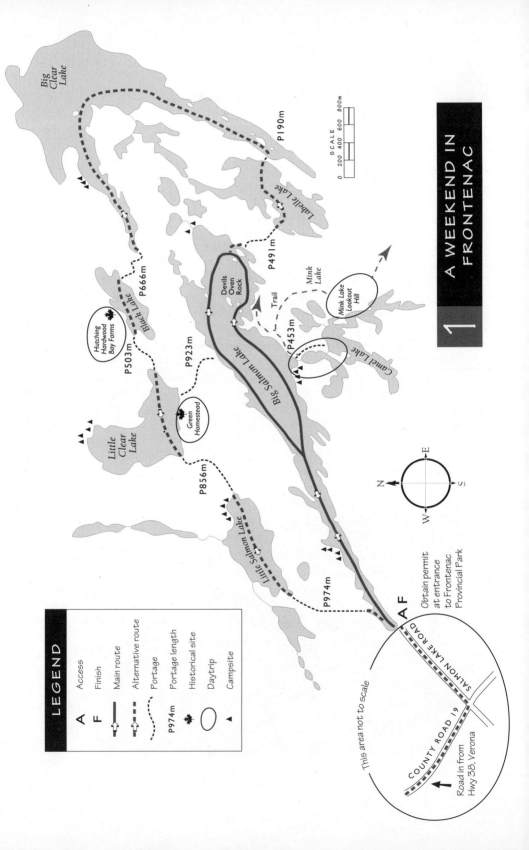

LEGEND

A	Access
F	Finish
	Main route
	Alternative route
	Portage
P974m	Portage length
	Historical site
	Daytrip
▲	Campsite

A WEEKEND IN FRONTENAC

1

Big Clear Lake

P190m

Labelle Lake

P491m

Mink Lake

Mink Lake Lookout Hill

P453m

Trail

Devils Oven Rock

Camel Lake

Big Salmon Lake

P666m

Black Lake

Hutching Hardwood Boy Farms

P503m

P923m

Green Homestead

Little Clear Lake

P856m

Little Salmon Lake

P974m

A F

Obtain permit at entrance to Frontenac Provincial Park

SALMON LAKE ROAD

COUNTY ROAD 19

Road in from Hwy 38, Verona

This area not to scale

SCALE

0 200 400 600 800m

N E W S

In the area of Little Clear Lake and Black Lake, north of Big Salmon Lake, traces of the Hutching, Hardwood Bay and Green farms can be found along a network of trails. The oldest settlement, the Hardwood Bay Farm, was originally established in 1842 to provide fresh hay for the horses and oxen of a local logging company. After the discovery of mica here in 1880, mining slowly replaced logging, and the construction of the two additional homesteads followed. The Hutching's shanty served as the local schoolhouse in the early 1900s.

Today the parkland's natural oasis is also worth exploring. A 453-metre portage lead directly from our campsite on Big Salmon Lake's southern shoreline to Camel Lake and its neighbouring bogs. The poorly drained wetlands provide excellent habitat for beaver, once seriously depleted in number during the early 1800s but reintroduced in the early 1940s by a family living to the west of the park.

A hike to the top of Mink Lake Lookout Hill makes another excellent day outing. The trail, also located on Big Salmon Lake's southern shoreline, meanders up the scoured slopes known to geologists as the Grenville Province of the Canadian Shield, a once-towering mountain range. The open ridges, made up mostly of diorite bedrock, have been scarred by three forest fires in the past 150 years, and provide only a thin layer of soil for sun-loving plants such as columbine and lowbrush blueberry.

Thinking back to the times spent crawling up and down Frontenac's rugged but beautiful ice-scoured landscape — stopping to show young Sarah a delicate yellow trout lily, and seeing her gawk at "Old Thor," the 1953 truck rusting away near the Green Homestead — my preconceived notions of all the hassles a child would bring to a canoe trip seem juvenile. In fact, exploring the semi-wilds of this natural environment park with an eighteen month old in tow, teaching her to love what I love, I found I was able to slow down and rediscover that canoe routes are not so much destinations as a way of life.

TIME:
1 to 2 days

DIFFICULTY:
Easy paddle for novice, especially for tripping with children.

PORTAGES:
0

FEE:
All vehicles, interior campers and day-users must obtain a permit at the trail centre. To camp on one of the interior sites, canoeists must have a valid permit; these are issued for a particular campsite for specific nights.

ALTERNATIVE ROUTES:
A short, weekend loop route can be made by way of Big Salmon Lake, Labelle Lake, Big Clear Lake, Black Lake, Little Clear Lake, Little Salmon Lake and back to Big Salmon Lake. However, the route has a total of six portages, three of which exceed 500 metres.

OUTFITTERS:
Canoe Outfitters
At the entrance to Frontenac Provincial Park
(613) 376-6220

FOR MORE INFORMATION:
Frontenac Provincial Park
Box 11
Sydenham, Ontario
K0H 2T0
(613) 376-3489

MAPS:
The Friends of Frontenac Park have produced an excellent map of the canoe routes and hiking trails within the provincial park.

Friends of Frontenac Park
Box 129
Sydenham, Ontario
K0H 2T0

TOPOGRAPHIC MAPS:
31 C/9, 31 C/10

Canoeists search the base of Mazinaw Rock for the 260 pictographs painted here hundreds of years ago.

2 The Mazinaw–Mississippi Route

The Mazinaw–Mississippi route, north of Kingston, may not be set in a pocket of forgotten wilderness, but there's something special about travelling through the same chunk of southern Canadian Shield that Algonquin shamans believed to be a gateway to the spirit world, where six members of the Group of Seven came to capture Canada on canvas, and where literary great W.O. Mitchell came to find his inspiration. I can't think of another canoe route where such a diverse group of influential Canadians has gathered in one place, and for that reason alone this trip is highly recommended.

The route begins at Mazinaw Lake's Bon Echo Provincial Park, located along Highway 41, three kilometres north of Cloyne. The park has a parking area and a place where canoeists can pitch a tent if they arrive at the access point late in the day. The park receives over 130,000 visitors a year, so it would wise to phone well ahead of time (613-336-2228) to book a reservation.

By staying the first night at the park you give yourself ample time come morning to paddle directly across the lake to Mazinaw Rock. There you can climb the metal staircase to the top of Mazinaw Rock, an incredible 100-metre-high precipice, or canoe along the base of the cliff to search out the 260 pictographs the Native people painted on the rock face hundreds of years ago.

The cliff was formed some time during the last million years when earthquakes fractured the surface rock, forcing half to rise and the other half to submerge.

The mystical character of the Mazinaw Rock has given rise to countless legends. Stories are still told of sacrificial virgins being tossed over the edge, Huron warriors ambushing raiding bands of Iroquois from high above the ridgetop, and mysterious creatures creeping up from the depths of the lake to devour unsuspecting canoeists. But one of the best-know stories is the tale of Meyer's Cave.

It is believed that Captain Meyer and a Métis named François travelled to the land of the Mississagagon (south of Mazinaw Lake) in search of the Algonquin's sacred treasure of silver. When they reached the Native village, the two cunning men passed a jug of rum around the fire, waited until the young men fell into a drunken slumber, and then kidnapped the old shaman of the village, forcing him to tell them the whereabouts of the treasure. The shaman lead them to a cave on top of Mazinaw Rock, where they packed away as much silver as they could carry. But as they climbed back down the cliff with their heavy burdens, the cave gods hurled spears of lightning from above, and the angry young men were waiting below to kill them.

It was Dr. Weston A. Price who, while on a canoe trip with college friends, named the area Bon Echo after hearing how clearly his voice reverberated from the cliff. Price returned in 1889 with his new bride to build the Bon Echo Inn, promoting the rock as "the Canadian Gibraltar." He sold the hotel in 1910 to Flora MacDonald Denison. Flora, and then later her son Merrill, turned the inn into a gathering place for the rich and famous, attracting such visitors as Ernest Hemingway and portrait photographer Yousuf Karsh.

The hotel was struck by lightning and burned to the ground in 1936. Merrill Denison gave the land to the government in 1959, and in 1965 Bon Echo Provincial Park was created.

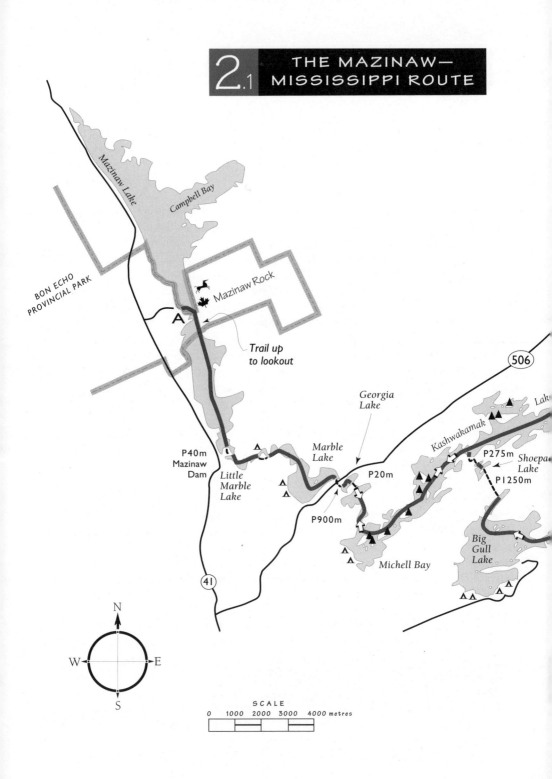

Mazinaw Lake

Campbell Bay

BON ECHO
PROVINCIAL PARK

Mazinaw Rock

A

Trail up
to lookout

Georgia
Lake

506

Kashwakamak Lak

P40m
Mazinaw
Dam

Little
Marble
Lake

Marble
Lake

P20m

P900m

P275m

Shoepa
Lake

P1250m

Michell Bay

Big
Gull
Lake

41

N

W ← → E

S

SCALE

0   1000   2000   3000   4000 metres

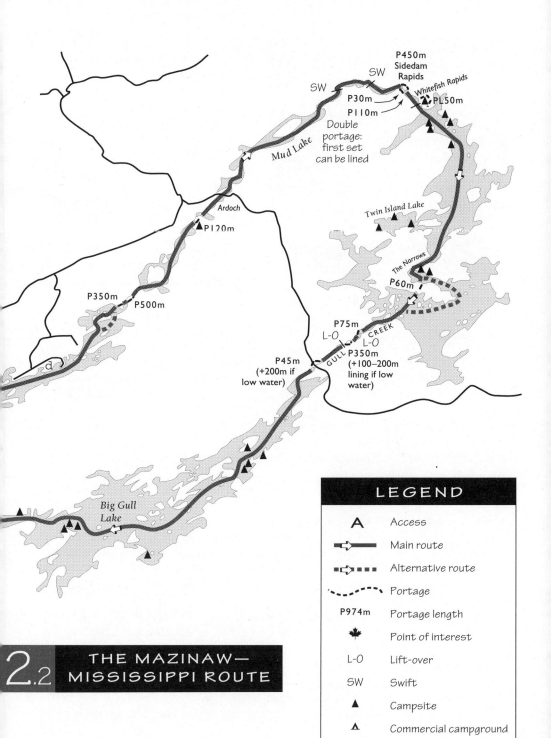

P450m
Sidedam
Rapids

SW

Whitefish Rapids

SW

P30m

PL50m

P110m

Double
portage:
first set
can be lined

Mud Lake

Twin Island Lake

Ardoch

P120m

The Narrows

P350m

P60m

P500m

P75m

L-O

GULL CREEK

L-O

P45m
(+200m if
low water)

P350m
(+100–200m
lining if low
water)

d

Big Gull
Lake

LEGEND

A   Access

Main route

Alternative route

Portage

P974m   Portage length

Point of interest

L-O   Lift-over

SW   Swift

▲   Campsite

⬮   Commercial campground

Pictograph

A perfect view is waiting for canoeists willing to climb up the steep trail to the top of Mazinaw Rock.

The park gives you a choice of two areas from which you can access the Mazinaw–Mississippi route. The main beach area offers lots of parking and a protective lagoon, but I find the secondary parking area is the better of the two put-in spots, as it is near the more isolated walk-in campsites maintained along the shoreline of Mazinaw Lake and away from the RVs and tent-trailers. If you're lucky enough to reserve one of these out-of-the-way sites, you can paddle directly from your campsite, heading over to the cliff face and then through the narrows toward the south half of Mazinaw Lake.

Lines from a poem by Walt Whitman have been chiselled into the hard granite on one section of the cliff just north of the narrows: "My foothold is tenon'd and mortised in granite / I laugh at what you call dissolution / and I know the amplitude of time." Flora MacDonald Denison, second owner of the Bon Echo Inn and devout fan of the American poet and conservationist, ordered the memorial a year before her death in 1921.

Paddling the length of Mazinaw Lake can be quite challenging if the winds pick up. Make sure to stay close to the shoreline until you reach the Mazinaw Lake Dam at the south end. To the right of the dam, look for the first portage, a 40-metre, well-marked trail with a steep slope at its far end.

This first set of rapids marks the beginning of the Mississippi River — not the "Mighty Mississippi," which flows 3,780 kilometres from Minnesota to the Gulf of Mexico, but Canada's miniature version, running only 201 kilometres from the Madawaska Highlands to the Ottawa River. No one is quite sure why or how the river got its name. "Mississippi" is used by Native people to describe the biggest river among surrounding rivers. With the Ottawa River nearby, however, this can hardly be the case here. Some historians conjecture that the name Mississippi was misinterpreted from the Algonquian word Mazinaw, or Mazinaw-eebi, meaning "painted image river."

You may have to line the section of river between the Mazinaw Lake Dam and Marble Lake when water levels are low. (Lining is guiding the canoe along from shore with ropes tied to bow and stern.) To the right, a 150-metre portage works around the worst of this shallow stretch. As you pass through along the southern shoreline, look up at the white marble outcrops that give Marble Lake its name. Gold is known to be hosted in marble, and it was this "gold-bearing" rock face that attracted miners to the area. However, only 50 ounces of the precious metal was taken from the crumpled rock, just east of here, between the late 1800s and early 1900s.

The river empties out of Marble Lake and into Georgia Lake just before the Highway 506 bridge. The rapids here were once navigated by a simple portage heading up and over the highway to the left. Unfortunately, a private landowner has now closed off the area (No Trespassing signs and barbed wire litter the site), and you must instead follow a route from the take-out on the left of the bridge by lining your canoe under the Highway 506 bridge, keeping close to the left bank.

If water levels are too high and the rocky ledge under the bridge is under water, you will be forced to carry your gear a somewhat greater distance by following Highway 506 west for 200 metres and then south, proceeding along Harlowe Road for 700 metres to the northern inlet of Kashwakamak Lake (formerly known as Long Lake).The put-in is to the left of the road.

The second set of rapids can be avoided downstream at the outlet of Georgia Lake. There is a 20-metre portage located to the right (directly under the hydro line), but lining the canoe down (guiding the canoe along from shore with ropes tied to bow and stern) may be your best bet.

A short paddle south through the narrows brings you to a T-intersection, where you will head east on Kashwakamak. It's best to make camp, however, before heading out along the elongated lake. Canoeists can choose from one of the two commercial campgrounds, Woodcrest Park (613-336-2966) and Camp Kashwakamak (613-479-2239) in the western bay, or choose a site on one of the Crown land islands ahead of where the steep walls of red rock tower along the north shore. To some, especially families out on their first canoe trip together, the luxury of having private parks situated along the way — complete with flush toilets and convenient stores — is a welcome option.

At Kashwakamak's easternmost end, a concrete dam marks the start of the first portage of the day. The 350-metre path, marked to the left, works its way alongside the Mississippi River, making a sharp turn three quarters of the way along as the river bends to the north. Directly across from the entry point of the previous portage, another path, 500 metres long and marked on the right bank, avoids a series of logjams in the river. The portage ends at an incredibly steep and muddy embankment, and even though canoeists have built a makeshift handrail, the going is still rough.

The river quickly opens up into a shallow marsh after the last portage, making its lazy way to the town of Ardoch and then eventually to Mud Lake. East of the Ardoch bridge, only a 120-metre portage along the right bank and two quick lift-overs are necessary. Avoid bogging down in the shallows immediately after the previously mentioned 500-metre portage and keep to the right-hand channel, especially at Mud Lake.

Left of the Mud Lake's centre island is a bed of wild rice said to have been planted years ago by an Algonquin woman, White Duck, of the Golden Lake Band. Her great-grandson, Harold Perry, has continued the faithful family tradition of watching over the wild rice — even after the famous wild rice war of Mud Lake. The dispute began when the Ministry of Natural Resources issued a harvesting permit to two men from Manitoba in 1979. The locals protested, and the Ministry sent in OPP helicopters and paddy wagons. When it was all over, a few of the demonstrators found themselves arrested and the two commercial harvesters quickly snuck out of town.

The Mississippi River gains momentum once again east of Mud Lake, just before flushing into Crotch Lake. The first whitewater stretch, Sidedam Rapids, is a double set and can be portaged either to the left for 450 metres along the Crotch Lake access road or by way of a path along the right bank. The portage on the south side of the river is approximately the same distance as the one on the north side. However, if your experience and skill permit, the first set of rapids can be run or lined, leaving you only a 110-metre carry.

Whitefish Rapids, the last set before Crotch Lake, comes shortly after. A 50-metre portage is marked to the left, but the rapid can be easily run at normal water levels.

Along this triple set of rapids, there are visible reminders of the days between the 1870s and 1880s when the river barons — Gilmour, Gillies, McLaren, Caldwell and the Canadian Lumber Company (a syndicate of lumbermen) — drove the great Mazinaw pines down the Mississippi to mills along the way or the entire distance to Quebec. It was here on the Mississippi that the famous feud between two of the major lumber companies on the river gave rise to a law making it illegal for anyone to monopolize a navigable waterway. Peter McLaren, who had constructed a series of dams, sluices and slides down the river, argued against Boyd Caldwell using the same route for his logs. Caldwell, who was granted river rights by the Ontario government and then continuously rejected by the federal government, was forced to cut his way through the series of dams and sneak his logs past McLaren's armed sentries under cover of darkness. The bitter dispute went on for ten years, with McLaren once holding Caldwell's logs back for three years in a row. Finally in 1884 the British Privy Council (acting as the final court of appeal for Canadians up until 1949) passed the province's Rivers and Streams Bill.

By the time the law was made, however, the big companies had all started leaving for greener pastures, deserting a barren landscape ravaged by fire after fire. The ashy earth was covered only by whitened tree trunks and black stumps, and lands here were called the "bald mountains" by the settlers once employed as shantymen who stayed behind to live off what was left.

Crotch Lake's rather inelegant name doesn't do it justice. In truth, apart from the Mazinaw Rock, it is the most scenic spot en route. The rocky shoreline, made up of what geologists call "muddy granite" (a whitish rock coloured by calcium feldspars), provides some excellent places to make camp, especially at the northernmost tip.

The lake is divided into an upper and lower section, and most of its shoreline is Crown land. The only major development is Tumblehome Lodge, to the south. The upper and lower sections of Crotch Lake are joined by a narrow channel. As you paddle south through the channel, the waterway will take a sudden turn east at a large peninsula. You can either make your way around, or choose to use an unmarked 60-metre portage located just behind a small pine-clad island as a shortcut. If you take the portage, however, you must search for a trail to the left near the put-in point to avoid the piles of logs washed up on shore.

The route now makes its way west. Locate Gull Creek at the end of the small southwestern inlet on Crotch Lake. A small falls marks the take-out for the next portage — a 75-metre path to the right of the cascade. How easily you travel up Gull Creek depends greatly on water levels. If the level is high, then a 300-metre portage on the left bank, possibly a short lift-over at a beaver dam, and to the right, a 45-metre carry over a road at Coxvale, will take you to Big Gull Lake. During a dry spell, however, you may have to line the canoe 100 to 200 metres past the 300-metre portage on the left bank, and extend the portage just before the road at least an additional 200 metres.

Winds on Big Gull Lake can be horrific. During a solo trip a few years back, I found myself fighting a tedious headwind while making my way to the Crown land campsites three quarters of the way along. The entire day was spent hop-skipping from one island to the next, trying to find protection from the waves that were rolling unimpeded across the long expanse of lake. By midafternoon I could go no further and found myself windbound on a tiny island in the bay east of Kirk Cove.

The winds continued to sculpt swells out on the lake well after nightfall. When I went to bed, listening to the gale flap the tent fly like a flag up on a pole, I began to wonder if I would ever get off the island. But at 3 a.m. I awoke to complete silence. The winds had mysteriously abated. One thing I've learned while travelling solo is to take full advantage of such a calm night, and under the cover of darkness I quickly packed up my gear and escaped off the island. The paddling was pleasant in the aftermath of the storm. By 5:30, rich morning light was breaking through the scattered clouds. I stopped to munch on a granola bar, lulled by the gentle rocking of the canoe, drifting along between a cluster of islands at the far western end of Big Gull Lake, near the mouth of a narrow channel. I was happy with my progress, but a slight breeze coming from the northwest reminded me that the morning calm never lasts long.

Northwest of the islands there is a marshy inlet lined with cattails, where a portage leads out of Big Gull Lake to Shoepack Lake. The take-out for the 1,250-metre path is on the north side of the inlet, just before a large patch of cattails. The beginning is steep, but the rest of the portage makes its way over a rolling landscape to the south shore of Shoepack Lake.

Another portage, to Kashwakamak Lake, is marked directly across from the previous one, to the right of a bay crowded with dead trees. Follow the 275-metre path to the road, and make a left. At the base of the hill, turn right onto the cottage road, and where the road forks, head straight through the centre to Kashwakamak Lake.

You can make your last campsite of the trip the same as the first, leaving day five to paddle north, back to Bon Echo Provincial Park, with enough time left to climb the Mazinaw Rock once more before driving back home. A perfect way to end a perfect trip.

TIME:
4 to 5 days

DIFFICULTY:
Apart from the possibility of high winds on Mazinaw, Kashwakamak and Big Gull Lakes, the route is relatively easy and makes an excellent introductory or family trip.

PORTAGES:
14

LONGEST PORTAGE:
1,250 metres

FEE:
Except for the first night spent at Bon Echo Provincial Park, campsites are on Crown land and a fee is required only if you are not a Canadian citizen.

ALTERNATIVE ACCESS:
Access can be had from a number of lodges, marinas and private campgrounds on Kashwakamak and Big Gull Lakes or the government launch on the south end of Crotch Lake.

ALTERNATIVE ROUTES:
By making use of alternative access points and not paddling the Mazinaw Lake section, canoeists can shorten the trip by a day and still paddle a complete loop.

OUTFITTERS:
Bon Echo Villa Marina & Tourist Facilities
R.R. 1
Cloyne, Ontario
K0H 1K0
(613) 336-2441

FOR MORE INFORMATION:
Ministry of Natural Resources
23 Spring Street,
Box 70
Tweed, Ontario
K0K 3J0
(613) 478-2330

Mississippi Valley Conservation Authority
Box 268
Lanark, Ontario
K0G 1K0
(613) 259-2421

MAPS:
The Ministry of Natural Resources in Tweed and the Mississippi Conservation Authority have produced canoe route guides to the area.

TOPOGRAPHIC MAPS:
31-C/14, 31-C/15

The Madawaska River is a paddler's paradise.

3 Paddling the Madawaska

In 1827, while exploring the Madawaska River for the possibility of establishing a naviga-
tional canal, Lieutenant J. Walpole recorded his observations: "The extraordinary rapidity
with which it descends into the Ottawa are circumstances which would render the operation,
if not infeasible, certainly enormously expensive and laborious." Also in the early 1800s, two
other noteworthy explorers — Lieutenant Catty and David Thompson — recorded that the
canal project was impractical due to the many rapids, falls and shallows along the Madawaska.
And so the river was left relatively abandoned, until a handful of lumber barons began con-
structing a series of booms, slides, piers and dams in 1836 in an attempt to control the river's
roaring current in order to harvest the thick stands of pine found upstream.

Nowadays, the same bellowing whitewater that kept the masses away from the
Madawaska attracts them in droves. Each year hundreds of canoeists come from all over to
enjoy paddling through the foam and froth, and instead of finding ways to control it, they
find ways to protect it

From its place of origin in Algonquin Park's Source Lake to the Ottawa River's Lac des
Chates at Arnprior (a distance of approximately 225 kilometres), the Madawaska descends
some 244 metres, drains an area of 4,992 square kilometres and, along the way, flows through
a dozen lakes. A paddler's paradise, to say the least.

Among the countless canoe routes that can be taken along the Madawaska — Source
Lake to the town of Whitney, Whitney to Bark Lake (part of the Upper Madawaska Provincial
Park), a day jaunt up the Little Madawaska, or afternoon playboating at Palmer Rapids — the
best weekend trip, in my opinion, can be found on the Lower Madawaska from Latchford
Bridge to Griffith (most of it a part of the Lower Madawaska Provincial Park).

On a two-day jaunt in mid-October, my regular canoe mate, Scott Roberts, and I were
able to reap the benefits of fall tripping: watching the morning sun paint the autumn colours;
feeling the crisp night air tempered by the warmth of an evening campfire; and most rewarding of all, the joy of having the river free of the regular season crowds.

Before our trip I contacted Don Adams (613-333-2240) to prearrange a shuttle service
from his place in Griffith. It was early Saturday morning when we pulled into Don's laneway,
south of the Highway 41 bridge. And after a brief introduction he squeezed into the front seat
with Scott and me and pointed the way to the Shroddar Road access point, west of the
Highway 515 bridge, near the town of Latchford Bridge.

After a thirty-minute drive we handed over the car keys to Don, pushed the canoe away
from the sandy banks of the Madawaska, and headed south through a shroud of morning
mist. The sun had diffused the vapour into ghost-shaped wisps by the time we reached
Aumonds Rapids — our first taste of whitewater, which begins with a double ledge separated
by a small island. Two more ledges followed in succession. All three sets of rapids can be
portaged by way of a side road running parallel to the river's left bank. Scott and I, however,
opted to run the entire stretch of Aumonds Rapids; there's nothing more exhilarating than to
start off a river trip by having your canoe pulled down the first descent — and then coming
out of the frothing surge of whitewater still afloat.

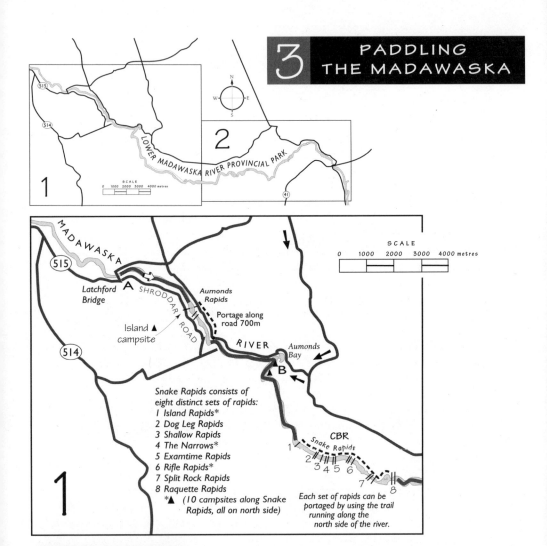

3 PADDLING THE MADAWASKA

Inset map 1

LOWER MADAWASKA RIVER PROVINCIAL PARK

SCALE
0 1000 2000 3000 4000 metres

N
W   E
S

Map 1

MADAWASKA

515

Latchford Bridge

A

SHRODDAR ROAD

Aumonds Rapids

Portage along road 700m

Island campsite ▲

514

RIVER

Aumonds Bay

B

SCALE
0 1000 2000 3000 4000 metres

Snake Rapids consists of eight distinct sets of rapids:
1 Island Rapids*
2 Dog Leg Rapids
3 Shallow Rapids
4 The Narrows*
5 Examtime Rapids
6 Rifle Rapids*
7 Split Rock Rapids
8 Raquette Rapids
*▲ (10 campsites along Snake Rapids, all on north side)

CBR
Snake Rapids
1
2 3 4 5 6
7
8

Each set of rapids can be portaged by using the trail running along the north side of the river.

1

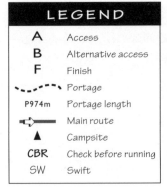

LEGEND

A	Access
B	Alternative access
F	Finish
- - - - -	Portage
P974m	Portage length
⬌	Main route
▲	Campsite
CBR	Check before running
SW	Swift

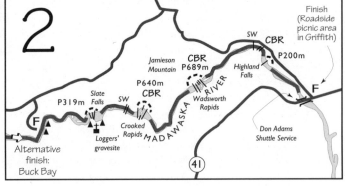

Map 2

2

Jamieson Mountain

CBR
P689m

SW   CBR

P200m

Finish (Roadside picnic area in Griffith)

P640m
CBR

Highland Falls

P319m

Slate Falls   SW

CBR

MADAWASKA   RIVER

Wadsworth Rapids

F

Alternative finish: Buck Bay

▲

Loggers' gravesite

Crooked Rapids

F

Don Adams Shuttle Service

41

Four kilometres from Aumonds Rapids is Aumonds Bay. The river splits here, forming a wide bay to the left (the site of the Aumonds Bay access point). The main channel continues to the right. This low-lying area is unlike the river's regular habitat. Red and white pine grow downstream, but species such as cedar, spruce and balsam make up most of tree cover here. Aumonds Bay also supports an extensive wetland, which is home to two rare orchids — showy lady's slipper and yellow lady's slipper — growing in a white cedar–tamarack bog to the south. Both of these species, which prefer the limestone substrates of Southern Ontario, are the only known rare orchids growing in the region.

Aumonds Bay also marks the beginning of the Lower Madawaska River Provincial Park. This 1,200-hectare park, which continues downstream to Griffith, is classified as a waterway park, and was created due to the river's extensive use by recreational canoeists.

The Aumonds Bay section ends downstream at the head of Snake Rapids, a 3.5-kilometre stretch of river consisting of eight distinct sets of rapids of varying levels of difficulty. Scott and I found that during moderate water levels, five of the eight sets of rapids (Dog Leg Rapids, Shallow Rapids, Exam Time Rapids, Split Rock Rapids and Raquette Rapids) could be graded Level 2. These had only high waves and the odd half-submerged boulder to pose any danger. The remaining three (Island Rapids, the Narrows and Rifle Chute), graded at Level 3, were beyond our whitewater skills, and we opted to use the portage. Take note, however, that each rapid comes complete with a portage (averaging 200 metres) marked on the left bank.

At every river constriction there are scenic campsites, also marked to the left. We stopped at the base of the eighth set, Raquette Rapids, for a late lunch, sipping on hot tea and recuperating after a series of blasting waves smacked cold water over our bow and nearly capsized us. It was late afternoon by the time we got the blood circulating through our veins once again, and though it was tempting to set up camp where we stood, we made a quick decision to paddle the remaining 5 kilometres of calm water to Slate Falls and make camp at the foot of the cascade.

We erected our tent on the centre island, just before the falls. It was a great campsite, but we later discovered that it is believed to be a Native burial ground. Had we known that at the time we would have, out of respect, stayed clear of the site.

Just before dusk Scott and I paddled across to the southern shoreline to gather firewood along the old portage. Because the original portage passed directly over etchings in the rock of the names and dates of loggers who died at Slate Falls, the Ministry of Natural Resources relocated the pathway across to the north side of the river (making it 319 metres in length).

Other century-old artifacts, weathered by time and damaged by thoughtless vandalism, can be found at almost every rapids or falls along the Madawaska, wherever log pins were hammered into granite and rock cribbing was constructed.

The present atmosphere of serenity and romance belies the origin of these relics of the past. Imagine a year's supply of logs being held back by a boom across the foot of Slate Falls to keep the timber from flushing down too quickly. And if a "jam" did occur, a volunteer would be lowered down to the single log holding back the tangle and would have to chop it away with an axe. Then, at the first sign of it giving way, the driver would head back to the safety of the shore, leaping from log to log. Some men made it. Some didn't.

There are countless stories told of how the spirits of the drowned log drivers can be heard shouting their haunting cries for help from above the surge of the river's current. All Scott and I heard while checking out the rock carvings, however, was the earsplitting crack of thunder from an approaching storm. That alone spooked us back to our campsite on the island, where we prepared for the worst by erecting a tarp over the fire circle and piling the wood we had gathered under the overturned canoe.

From our vantage point at the centre of the river we could see the black clouds, not so much gathering in the sky as flying across it, carrying a sheet of hail and hurling it down at the distant hills. We fed the fire and crouched close by its warmth, as if it would ward off the elements, as, for an hour, our small, vulnerable island campsite was engulfed in the noise and power of the storm.

By 10 p.m. the storm clouds had lifted, unveiling an incredible starlit sky. We doused the fire and zipped ourselves into our mummy bags, feeling that our escape from the cold downpour had been nothing short of a miracle. The air was crisp and cool early the next morning, compelling us to rekindle the campfire and dance a jig around the island in an attempt to keep warm. Eventually, the heat of the morning sun burned away the frost, and after finishing a second cup of camp coffee (spiked with a shot of Irish Cream) we stashed our wool toques into our packs and paddled across to the north shore. From here we portaged to the base of Slate Falls, where after rushing headlong over a garden of rock the river widens and slows down to a meandering stroll.

Downstream from Slate Falls lies Crooked Rapids. A 640-metre portage is marked on the left bank, near the end of a runnable swift that comes before the major section of whitewater. A large section of the portage follows along the Crooked Rapid Access Road, providing a fairly easy path to carry your gear over. Still, the rapid itself can be run if care is taken to scout the best route through the labyrinth of islands. During moderate water levels the left channel is best, as there are dangerous haystack waves near the base of the channel to the right. The right, however, is more direct and has fewer boulders to manoeuvre around.

Next is Wadsworth Rapids, complete with a 689-metre portage also along the left bank. After checking out this well-worn path that runs directly along the edge of a cliff, Scott and I chose to run the rapid, and by lining and eddy-hopping we found paddling the stretch of whitewater was far easier than carrying over on the lengthy portage.

Before reaching Wadsworth Rapids, we also took time out to scramble up Jamieson Mountain, located on the north side of the river. From the crest of the hill we were able to get a good view of the landscape we were travelling through — a breathtaking vista of miniature mountains carpeted in lush autumn colours.

Continuing down the river, past Wadsworth Rapids, there are only three more noteworthy sets of whitewater before you reach the take-out point at the government park, on the left bank, just before the Highway 41 bridge in Griffith.

The first whitewater occurs where a large island splits the river. You can take the left or right channel around the island and choose either to run, line or wade the shallow swift. The next rapid is found shortly after a bend in the river. An unmarked portage (approximately 200 metres) is located to the left, but the rapid can be easily run during low and moderate water levels.

The last challenge is a major drop, called Highland Falls. An unmarked portage can be found along the left bank, but the path runs through private land, and it may be best to line your canoe down to the right or carry directly over the centre island at the foot of the falls. Of course, if your skill is up to snuff you could choose to run the cascade (graded at Level 4).

The Lower Madawaska River Provincial Park is a waterway park used extensively by recreational canoeists.

Scott and I decided to run Highland Falls. I'm not sure why. Perhaps our egos had been boosted by running the rapids upstream without a single mishap. The moment the current grabbed hold of our canoe and pulled us downhill with it, we knew we were way out of our league.

We chose the right channel. Halfway through our predestined route we found ourselves being pulled off course by the gushing water. Our paddle strokes quickly became futile, and the river soon had complete control over our boat. It was like dropping down a roller coaster; all we could do was to hold on and wait until the ride was over.

Seconds later we opened our eyes and found ourselves floating upright at the base of the falls, the canoe a third full of water and us soaked to the ears. By the time we reached the take-out we were chilled to the bone, shivering uncontrollably. Don Adams was waiting for us at the government parking lot, with the car heater going full tilt.

A half an hour later we found ourselves warm and dry, sipping hot coffee at a local diner and relishing the fact that we had completed the river without once being tossed into the drink. We acted like a couple of ecstatic schoolboys, knowing in our hearts that it was more luck than skill that brought us down that river.

TIME:
2 days

DIFFICULTY:
All rapids can be portaged. However, canoeists should have a moderate to high level of experience in paddling whitewater.

PORTAGES:
14

LONGEST PORTAGE:
689 metres

FEE:
The Madawaska Provincial Park is an unmaintained waterway park and therefore no camping permit need be purchased.

ALTERNATIVE ACCESS:
Aumonds Bay and Buck Bay access points can be reached by way of a bush road that runs parallel to the north side of the river, west of Highway 41 from Griffith to Quadeville.

ALTERNATIVE ROUTE:
By accessing the river at the Ministry of Natural Resources put-in at Aumonds Bay and ending at Buck Bay, one can experience the major set of rapids on a one-day trip.

OUTFITTERS:
Multi-Trek Canadian Explorers Rentals/Outfitting
1180 Tawney Road
Ottawa, Ontario
K1G 1B7
(613) 748-6165

Don Adams Shuttle Service
Griffith, Ontario
(613) 333-2240

Madawaska Shuttle Service
Griffith General Store
General Delivery
Griffith, Ontario K0J 2R0
(613) 333-5555

FOR MORE INFORMATION:
Ministry of Natural Resources
Pembroke District Office
Box 220
Riverside Drive
Pembroke, Ontario
K8A 6X4
(613) 732-3661

TOPOGRAPHIC MAPS:
31 F/3, 31 F/6

Early morning at Slate Falls, Madawaska River.

A short trail from the Achray Road to the north rim of the Barron Canyon provides an excellent view of the next day's canoe route.

4 The Barron River Canyon
A Paddle Through Time

The Barron River (named after Augustus Barron, a member of the House of Commons, in 1890), is clearly the gem of Algonquin Provincial Park's east side. The waterway is lined with steep walls of hard, crystalline rock that tower far above the water, 100 metres at the highest point, isolating the river and helping to defend its solitude.

The cliffs, however, only seem to dominate the primitive landscape; they are themselves dominated by the river, and were sculpted by the waters of historic Lake Algonquin some 11,000 years ago, toward the end of the last ice age. It took only a few centuries for the glacial meltwater, once equivalent in volume to a thousand Niagara Falls, to retreat northward from what geologists called the Fossmill Outlet to a lower geological fault — the Lake Nipissing–Mattawa channel, reducing the Barron River to a mere trickle.

To reach the canyon (marked as Access Point 22 on the Algonquin Provincial Park map), turn left off Highway 17 (approximately 9 kilometres west of Pembroke) on County Road 26. Then, after only 300 metres, take the first right at the Achray Road and drive 26 kilometres to Sand Lake Gate at the park boundary. Once you have received your camping permit (you may want to phone ahead to reserve), continue for another 19 kilometres and turn left on a side road leading to the Achray Campground at the southeast tip of Grand Lake. On your way to Achray you may want to make a quick stop at the Barron Canyon Trail (8 kilometres before the turn-off to the Achray Campground). The 1.5-kilometre loop trail will give you an excellent view of the next day's canoe route from the canyon's north rim.

If you arrive late in the day, the campground on Grand Lake is an excellent place to spend the first night of your trip. If time permits, take a quick paddle after dinner to the east end of the lake to explore one of Tom Thompson's sketching sites. In 1916, a year before the Canadian artist mysteriously drowned on Algonquin's Canoe Lake, Thompson produced the gloomy *Jack Pine* from the small point of land on the left, just before the lake narrows and leads to the portage to Stratton Lake. The conifer had been scarred by fire when Thompson painted it, but managed to stand erect up until the late 1970s, when it finally toppled to the ground and was used for firewood by a group of campers.

Head out early if you stayed at the Achray Campground your first night, portaging 30 metres into Stratton Lake, and then after paddling the full length of

Canoeists load up at the Achray access point.

4 THE BARRON RIVER CANYON
A PADDLE THROUGH TIME

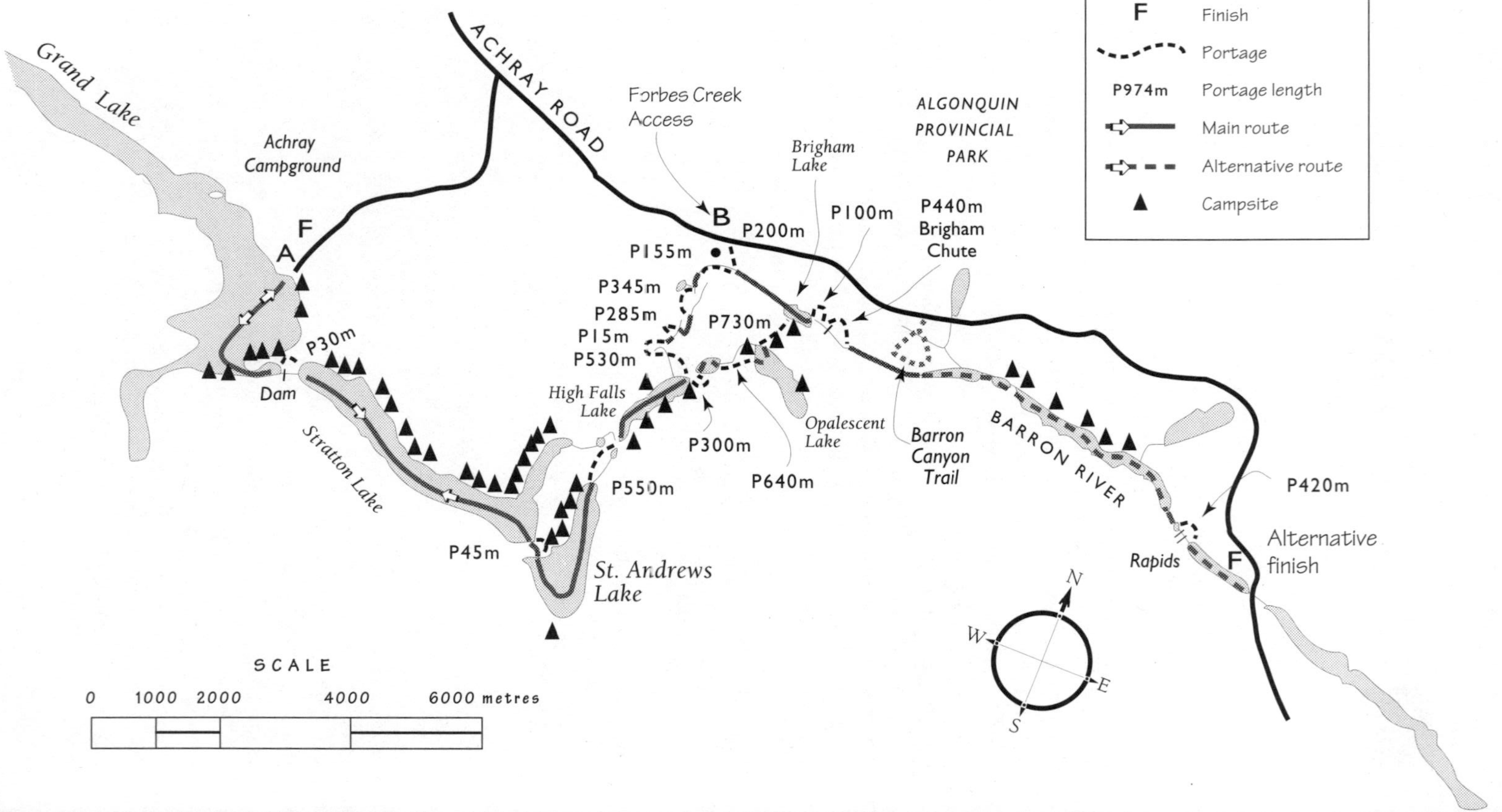

LEGEND

A	Access
	Alternative access
B	
F	Finish
	Portage
P974m	Portage length
	Main route
	Alternative route
▲	Campsite

Grand Lake

Achray Campground

ACHRAY ROAD

Forbes Creek Access

ALGONQUIN PROVINCIAL PARK

Brigham Lake

P440m Brigham Chute

P100m

P200m

P155m

P345m
P285m
P15m
P530m

P730m

High Falls Lake

P300m

P640m

Opalescent Lake

Barron Canyon Trail

BARRON RIVER

P550m

St. Andrews Lake

P45m

Stratton Lake

Dam

P30m

Rapids

P420m

Alternative finish

SCALE

0   1000   2000   4000   6000 metres

N E S W

Stratton, portage 45 metres into St. Andrews Lake. From here it's best to set up a base camp and make the trip to the Barron River Canyon into a daytrip.

From St. Andrews Lake, take the 550-metre portage into High Falls Lake. The trail is marked in St. Andrews' northeastern bay.

From the northern tip of High Falls Lake, stay with the river by following the 530-metre portage to the left. Six more portages (the longest is 345 metres and all are marked on the left bank except the fifth) lead you into Brigham Lake. Directly across the small pond, two more portages (100 metres and 440 metres), marked on the left, take you around Brigham Chute.

What lies ahead is spectacular. Precipitously cut cliffs, where bright orange lichen (xanthoria) and miniature, lime-loving encrusted saxifrage plants are rooted in the damp crevices, create a canyon so primeval that you can imagine you have travelled back in time.

From here the river is in no great hurry and you can drift slowly between the granite walls, gawking up at soaring ravens and red-tailed hawks that nest high up on the rock cliffs. And when it's time to head back to base camp, rather than lug your canoe up the series of cascades, take the 730-metre portage on the southwestern shore of Brigham Lake into Opalescent Lake, and then head directly across that lake to a 640-metre portage, followed by a short 300-metre portage, to reach familiar High Falls Lake.

Once back at St. Andrews Lake, bake up some biscuits, brew up a pail of camp coffee, and gather by the glowing embers of the evening fire to rekindle the day's events on the ancient Barron River.

TIME:
2 to 3 days

DIFFICULTY:
Novice

PORTAGES:
19

LONGEST PORTAGE:
730 metres

FEE:
An interior camping permit must be purchased at the Sand Lake Gate, and if you choose to spend the first night at the Achray Campground on Grand Lake you must also obtain a campsite permit.

ALTERNATIVE ACCESS:

The Barron River can also be accessed directly where the Achray Road crosses over the river (parking is on your left), or close to where the Forbes Creek enters into the Barron River, at a small parking lot a short drive beyond the Barron River Trail access point.

ALTERNATIVE ROUTES:
By making use of the alternative access points, canoeists can either paddle directly up the Barron River from the Achray Road bridge or, by leaving a pick-up vehicle at the bridge, paddle downstream from the Forbes Creek access point.

OUTFITTERS:
Algonquin Portage
R.R. 6
Pembroke, Ontario

K8A 6W7
(613) 735-1795

FOR MORE INFORMATION:
Algonquin Provincial Park
Ministry of Natural Resources
Box 219
Whitney, Ontario
K0J 2M0
(705) 633-5572 (information)
(705) 633-5538 (reservations)

MAPS:
The Friends of Algonquin have produced an excellent map of Algonquin's interior.

TOPOGRAPHIC MAPS:
31 F/13

With spring tripping come soggy portages (Algonquin's Daisy Lake).

5 Algonquin's Wild West

I can't think of a better way to celebrate the coming of spring than a canoe trip in Ontario's world-famous Algonquin Provincial Park. The moment the ice is out and trout season is open, my regular canoe mates and I head for the park's interior to endure cold nights, soggy portages, bloodthirsty blackflies, and freak snowstorms, all in the hope of spotting a moose, smelling the sweet aroma of spring flowers or, better yet, hooking into a trophy-size trout.

Throughout the years we've altered our route in search of bigger fish and less crowded portages. However, we've made the majority of our outings in the west side of the park's 7,600 square kilometres. This lake-covered highland, from which three major rivers flow (the Petawawa, Nippissing and Tim), is a haven for lake trout and the pink-fleshed brook trout.

From Access 3 on Magnetawan Lake, a perfect four- to five-day loop can be had, with the added bonus of avoiding any portage longer than 900 metres — something I'm sure that regular park users would agree is hard to come by in Algonquin's interior.

To reach Magnetawan Lake, take Highway 11, north of Huntsville, and make a right onto Highway 518 at Emsdale. Follow 518 to the town of Kearney, and then keeping left where the road splits, continue for another 14.4 kilometres until you reach the gravelled Forestry Tower Road. Make a right here, following the rough road for 13 kilometres to the Ministry of Natural Resources office.

After picking up your vehicle and interior camping permit, follow the gravel road, keeping to the right, for another 12.2 kilometres to the parking area on the northwest shore of Magnetawan Lake. Don't even think about arriving at the Ministry office without phoning months before (705-633-5538) to reserve your route. The daily quota for canoeists entering the park from this access point is only fifteen. If the quota is filled, consider starting your trip from Access 4 (Rain Lake).

From the parking lot a short path leads to the dock on Magnetawan Lake. After you lock up your vehicle and load your gear into the canoe, a quick paddle directly across from the dock will take you to the first portage (135 metres) of your trip, leading into Hambone Lake.

Keeping to the shoreline to your right on Hambone Lake, paddle into the second elongated bay; there, where the waterway narrows, a quick 55-metre portage on the left avoids a shallow section. In high water, however, you can usually paddle straight through if the bow person keeps an eye out for hidden rocks.

The channel opens up into a small pond, where the next portage (420 metres) is marked directly across. The rugged path leads the way to Daisy Lake, working its way over a mountain of rock, and then down to a makeshift dock sunk into smelly swamp ooze.

On Daisy Lake, head south out of the bay, and then east toward the sandy shallows where the Petawawa River begins. A 135-metre portage to the left is necessary to avoid the place where the river drops over a rock shelf. It flows into the narrow, meandering waterway lined with alder, dogwood and patches of tamarack.

LEGEND

A	Access
B	Alternative access
F	Finish
⌐⌐⌐	Portage
P974m	Portage length
❧	Historical site
⟹	Main route
⟹▪▪▪	Alternative route
▲	Campsite
✲	Marshy area

To Tim Lake

Gatehouse

Butt Lake

Hambone Lake

PETAWAWA RIVER

Little Misty Lake

Misty Lake

P935m

P450m

Portage into Mocassin Lake

P765m

Alternative portage to Misty Lake from Timberwolf Lake

P135m

P55m

P 135 m

F A

P 420 m

Magnetawan Lake

Daisy Lake

Shortly after, another portage (450 metres) is marked along the left bank. Some canoeists choose to shorten the carry by paddling a 200-metre section between a set of double rapids. Once the canoe is balanced over my shoulders, however, I prefer to keep going to the bitter end.

Downriver from the put-in of the last portage, the river starts to become less constricted, and is free of logjams and beaver dams. Eventually it opens up into Little Misty Lake, where you may see some of Algonquin's four thousand moose browsing in the shallows. The number of moose sighted depends greatly on the time of year. Usually we spot a young bull, or, if we're lucky, a cow and her calf. On one particular trip, the salt-enriched aquatic plants had just begun to sprout, drawing the moose to the water's edge, and we counted a grand total of twenty-nine moose feeding from the weedy effluent.

The first moose sighting of that same trip was the most memorable. Scott, my canoe partner, and I had stopped paddling for a swig of juice and a handful of GORP (good old raisins and peanuts) while our friends went ahead. After a few minutes had passed we decided we had better push on if we were to catch up with the others. Just around the next bend, however, we found our companions' path blocked by a odd-looking moose wading in midstream.

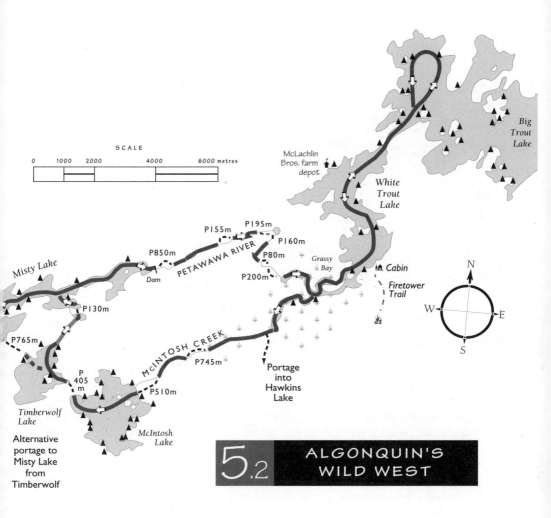

The beast refused to move for at least twenty minutes. Of course, the moment I decided to take advantage of the situation and unpack my camera, the moose sprang out of the water and into the bush. Later that same day, we overheard some other canoeists telling a similar tale of a half-crazed moose blocking their path at the same spot on the river. Except they managed to shoot an entire role of film before the moose stepped aside.

At the far end of Little Misty Lake, the longest portage en route (935 metres) heads over a steep knoll carpeted of maple, beech and birch (typical forest cover of the western uplands), to the northwestern bay of Misty Lake.

Misty Lake is an excellent place to make camp for the first night. My favourite site is on the north side of the large island. It's well protected from the winds that always seem to pick up on Misty, and has an excellent rock outcrop from which you can cast a line for trout cruising the shallows come dusk. Day two is spent back on the Petawawa to Big Trout Lake, the centrepiece of Algonquin's interior. The river flushes out at the end of Misty Lake's elongated eastern inlet. Here you will find a 850-metre portage marked to the left, starting up a steep and slippery embankment. Two short sets of rapids, the first with a 155-metre portage

Lost again in Algonquin's Grassy Bay.

to the left and the second, a 195-metre portage to the right, are also located not far downriver. Of the two sets, only the first can be run.

The river once again slows its pace, and then suddenly takes a sharp turn to the south at a scenic double chute. A steep, 160-metre portage on the right heads directly overland, well below the rough water, and you must paddle a good distance upstream from the put-in if you wish to view the base of the run.

High cliffs with small pockets of white pine growing out of the thick stands of black spruce now begin to interrupt the low, swampy banks. A dramatic falls follows the last cascade of water upriver; there is an 80-metre portage to the left. And directly after, marked to the right, you must follow a 200-metre portage to avoid the last set of rapids of the day, where the Petawawa flows into the swampy shallows of Grassy Bay.

It's become a ritual for me and my canoe companions to cast a line for speckled trout at the base of each rapids along the entire stretch of the Petawawa. If the fish are biting, we're pretty much guaranteed a "brookie" on the first cast. One can imagine, then, the competitive nature of the group as we hurry over the portage in the race to be the first to fish the hole. My canoe partner, Scott Roberts, has a special knack to beat everyone to the punch. But after he had caught and released over half-a-dozen good-sized specks, the group decided to allow Mike, who had yet to catch anything on all of our previous trips, to have first dibs on the last hole of the day.

Mike and his canoe mate, Doug, pushed off from shore to reach the centre of the deep pool. We all stood and watched with anticipation as Mike's lure slapped the surface of the water and then sank down beneath the soft current — all of us except for Scott, that is. The scoundrel had grabbed his rod and reel from his pack, snuck through the brush, and he took a cast from shore.

Before we could protest his unsportsmanlike conduct, both Mike and Scott hooked into a fish. Sadly, however, Mike's bad luck had prevailed. While Scott proudly displayed a two-pound brook trout, Mike was busy wrestling with his lure, which had deeply embedded itself into his catch — a slimy sucker!

From the base of the last rapids, head out into the twisting channel of Grassy Bay, which eventually splits east and west. Head east into the expanse of White Trout Lake and either make camp here, or paddle across and through the connecting channel to Big Trout Lake. Big Trout has countless island campsites, but in the past our group has chosen always to camp on the smaller White Trout Lake, spending an entire day either exploring the old McLachlin farming depot used by loggers in the early 1900s or hiking up to the site of the abandoned firetower. The farm post can be found along the shore to the northeast, and the tower trail begins at the south of White Trout Lake, where a ranger cabin can be sighted in a clearing. The tower has been recently dismantled by park staff for safety reasons, but the one-and-a-half-hour hike to the peak is still worthwhile.

After a rest day exploring White Trout Lake or fishing for monster lake trout on Big Trout Lake, the next two days are spent looping back to the access point on Magnetawan Lake. To return, enter back into the swampy maze of Grassy Bay from White Trout Lake's southeastern tip, and instead of paddling up the Petawawa River, head directly west into the main channel of the labyrinth.

Even with provincial park signs posted on stumps to point the right way through Grassy Bay, it's not difficult to find yourself questioning your whereabouts every ten minutes. With every channel looking the same, you will probably end up unpacking your map and compass now and then to locate the main throughway to McIntosh Creek.

Grassy Bay and McIntosh Creek join by way of a 745-metre portage criss-crossing the creek along its entire length. You must lift over a number of beaver dams before you reach a second portage. This 510-metre path climbs out of the lowlands and up into McIntosh Lake.

From McIntosh's northwestern bay a 405-metre portage connects you with Timberwolf Lake (an excellent spot for lake trout). And finally, to get back to Misty Lake from Timberwolf, choose either to take a soggy 765-metre portage at the north end or paddle northeast up a weedy inlet to a shorter 130-metre portage.

The loop ends on Misty Lake, where you will spend your last night in Algonquin's interior. The rest of the route retraces itself back up the Petawawa River to Daisy Lake, and then north to Hambone and west to the Magnetawan access point.

TIME:
4 to 5 days

DIFFICULTY:
Moderate to novice tripping experience.

PORTAGES:
22

LONGEST PORTAGE:
935 metres

FEE:
An interior camping permit must be purchased at the access point gatehouse before you set out into the interior of Algonquin Provincial Park.

ALTERNATIVE ACCESS:
If Access Point 3 is filled to capacity, canoeists can head out from the Rain Lake access point (Access Point 4 on the Algonquin Provincial Park Canoe Map).

ALTERNATIVE ROUTE:
The route can be shortened to a weekend trip by paddling only into Misty Lake and back.

OUTFITTERS:
Rickwards Small Motors
Box 224
Kearney, Ontario
P0A 1M0
(705) 636-5956

FOR MORE INFORMATION:
Algonquin Provincial Park
Ministry of Natural Resources
Box 219
Whitney, Ontario
K0J 2M0
(705) 633-5572 (information)
(705) 633-5538 (reservations)

MAPS:
Ministry of Natural Resources Algonquin Provincial Park Canoe Map

TOPOGRAPHIC MAPS:
31 E/10, 31 E/15

Canal Rapids, Magnetawan River.

6 The Magnetawan River Loop

My first time ever paddling the Magnetawan River loop I made the mistake of heading out in mid-June, when blackflies, mosquitoes and deer flies joined forces to plague each and every portage. John Glasgow (my canoe companion that week) had been so badly bitten by insects (I counted a total of twenty-two bug bites on John's left kneecap) that he looked like a walking pincushion. The insanely long portages en route (the longest measuring 2,285 metres) were blocked with either mud puddles or sharp granite slopes. And, to make matters worse, a pre-summer heat wave hit the area; with the humidity, temperatures soared as high as 40 degrees Celsius (112 F). By the time the ordeal was over we both agreed wholeheartedly that our first trip would be the last. Three months later, however, John and I found ourselves talking over the trip at a local bar, declaring how cheated we both felt after it was all over. We agreed that if it wasn't for the excessive heat and bugs we encountered along the way, the Magnetawan itself wouldn't have been a total disaster.

So, believe it or not, we gave the route a second chance, this time in mid-September when the air was cool and the portages were free of bugs. And our second time around, we came out unscathed. In fact, John and I had such a good trip that we can honestly say that the Magnetawan loop, when paddled at the right time of the year, of course, is at the top of the list when it comes to Ontario's canoe routes.

The Magnetawan River loop has three possible access points: Naiscoot Lake and Harris Lake, both off Highway 69, and Wahwashkesh Lake, off Highway 124 and Highway 520.

John and I chose the Wahwashkesh Lake access point. The public boat launch can be reached by taking Highway 124, turning north onto Highway 520 just east of Dunchurch, and turning north again onto Wahwashkesh Lake Road (before the town of Whitestone). The parking lot and dock site are 8.9 kilometres along this road, just past Linger Long Lodge.

Wahwashkesh Lake is a large lake with countless islands and bays that can easily confuse any navigator. To reach the Magnetawan River, paddle to the northwest bay (Deep Bay).

The first and longest portage of the trip is downriver at Canal Rapids. Where the river forks before the rapid, follow the right-hand inlet. The portage begins just right of the Deep Bay Hunt Club dock. It then follows an old tote road built by loggers in 1868 and ends where a bridge crosses the river.

Looking upstream from the bridge you can catch a good glimpse of Canal Rapids, where canyon walls 15 metres sheer on either side direct the flow of the river over a series of rock staircases.

A short distance downstream is Graves Rapids. Local people say there is a graveyard here for the log drivers who drowned in the rapids. The Magnetawan Archives contain this description from James MacArthur, a lumberman and settler of the South Magnetawan, as he saw the site in 1926: "Not far above the shallows where the creek enters the Magnetawan, is a plot of ground on a sunny slope, with a cedar fence surrounding it. Here are the graves of two river drivers drowned in the canal thirty years ago [1896] running a pointer boat through. The spot is tended to each spring by the passing drives. Gone are most of the curios left by fellow workers — the corked shoes, pipes, broken watch cases, and other knickknacks. The carved doves that rested over the head of the pieces, miniature 'peaveys' and pike poles, marauding tourists have lifted."

6.1 THE MAGNETAWAN RIVER LOOP

MAGNETAWAN

Island Lake

Stovepipe Rapids

P390m

P45m

Mountain Chute

Thirty Dollar Rapids

RIVER

Three Snye Rapids

P2380m

P1370m

P190m on left

P293m

2 L-O on left

SOUTH BRANCH

Harris Lake

HARRIS LAKE ROAD

TRANS-CANADA HIGHWAY

B

Harris Lake Dam

Big Bay

Timber Wolf Lake

Miskokway Lake

B

F

Alternative finish

Naiscoot Lake

P480m

P825m

Little Wilson Lake

Wilson Lake

69

P70m

P250m

P39m

Clear Lake (Wassagami Lake)

Lone Tree Lake

P8m

P390m

Evans Lake

P450m

Naiscoot Lake

Little Wilson Lake

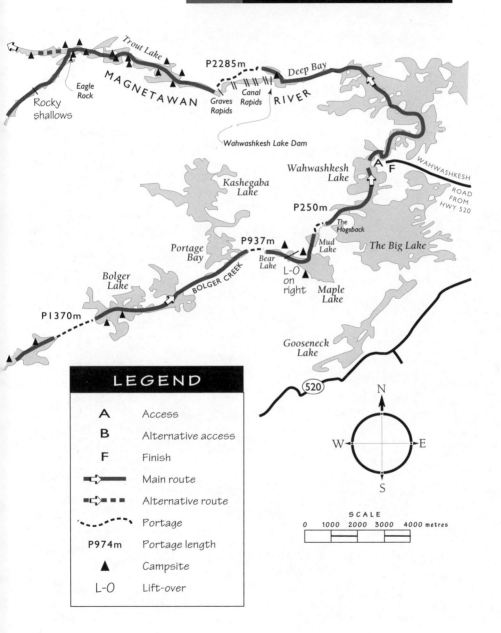

Trout Lake

P2285m

Deep Bay

Eagle Rock

MAGNETAWAN

Rocky shallows

Graves Rapids

Canal Rapids

RIVER

Wahwashkesh Lake Dam

Wahwashkesh Lake

A F

WAHWASHKESH ROAD FROM HWY 520

Kashegaba Lake

P250m

The Hogsback

The Big Lake

Portage Bay

P937m

Mud Lake

BOLGER CREEK

Bear Lake

L-O on right

Maple Lake

Bolger Lake

P1370m

Gooseneck Lake

520

LEGEND

A	Access
B	Alternative access
F	Finish
⇨━━	Main route
⇨■ ■ ■	Alternative route
⸜⸝⸜	Portage
P974m	Portage length
▲	Campsite
L-O	Lift-over

N
W — E
S

SCALE
0   1000   2000   3000   4000 metres

Campsite on Miskokway Lake, Magnetawan River.

Canoeists have three options at Graves Rapids: continue along the tote road for another 500 metres, paddle from the bridge to the foot of the rapid and use a separate 200-metre portage found to the right, or if your whitewater skills are up to it, cautiously run the set.

West of Graves Rapids is Trout Lake, an incredible, scenic lake with a number of perfect campsites, each with rock outcrops and lush canopies of red and white pine. I can guarantee that spending your first night camped on the lake will be one of the highlights of the entire trip.

From Trout Lake the regular route follows the South Branch. But if you're in the mood for more long, wet, muddy portages, it is possible to extend the trip for another day by continuing to paddle west across Island Lake, portaging 2,380 metres around Thirty Dollar Rapids (so named after an entire drive of logs jammed and cost the dollar-a-day loggers a month's pay), and then looping back to the South Branch by way of a 1,370-metre portage.

The added day brings you through some major historic sites. You may find the long portages too gruelling, however, and opt to keep to the main route to the south. Look for Eagle Rock, a prominent cliff marking the entrance to the narrow inlet leaving Trout Lake.

Many riffles, too minor to be called rapids, speed your progress to the spot where the hydro line crosses the river. The rocky shoreline smooths out here, and clumps of lush white birch begin to replace the red and white pine. Depending on water levels, you may have to make a double lift-over where the current flushes over two rock ledges in succession, directly below the power lines. And shortly downstream, a 293-metre portage on the right bank must be taken to avoid a stunted cascade.

The landscape regains its rugged appeal south of the Canadian National Railway bridge. Here, where the waterway forks, the South Magnetawan River travels west toward Harris Lake; to the south, where you will be paddling, is Big Bay.

The next portage (70 metres) is located along the eastern shoreline, just before the southern tip of Big Bay. Wooden steps have been put in place at the take-out to help you scramble up a steep slope. Keep a sharp look out for where the path forks. A well-maintained trail continues to the left. That's not the way you want to go. Trust me! I've learned by mistake. Follow the faint path to the right to Clear Lake (Wassagami Lake).

From Clear Lake a series of six small lakes follow, each one enclosed by walls of hard granite and separated by short, but steep and rugged portages. The third lake (Lone Tree Lake) and the sixth lake (Evans Lake) are miniature versions of Trout Lake, providing yet again picture-perfect campsites.

Special note should be made of the 390-metre portage into Evans Lake. I'm sure that during low water the entire portage is necessary, but when John and I paddled the route we shortened the path by at least 200 metres by navigating the shallow creek.

From Evans Lake's southwestern shore, a good 450-metre portage takes you to where Naiscoot Lake and Wilson Lake join. The route heads east down almost the entire length of Wilson Lake, until another portage, located on the northern shoreline, heads overland to a small unnamed lake.

It was on this particular steep portage that both John and I came to the logical conclusion that the map we were following, produced by the Ministry of Natural Resources (MNR) and entitled *Magnetawan River Canoe Route*, was somewhat inaccurate in its portage measurements. The MNR pamphlet recorded the path out of Wilson Lake as 825 metres in length. It seemed to us more like 1,000 metres. To make matters worse, the even longer portages that follow also appeared to be incorrectly reported.

Trout Lake comes complete with perfect campsites, each with rock outcrops and lush canopies of red and white pine.

On the left-hand shore in the unnamed lake's northern bay, a 480-metre (600 metre?) portage works down a precipitous slope to Miskokway Lake. Paddle east across the length of Miskokway to yet another portage. The 1,370-metre (2,000 metre?) trail begins at a local hunt club's boat launch area, crosses over a small creek, and then follows a rough road all the way to the Bolger Lake boat launch. The halfway mark along the portage is at a hydro line, just after a second dirt road crosses your path.

John and I remember this particular portage extremely well. It was here, during our trip in mid-June, that we were attacked by literally hundreds of bloodthirsty bugs. By the time we reached Bolger Lake, John required immediate first aid (a yellowish pus had begun oozing out of his bites), and I went into a uncontrollable coughing fit and eventually vomited out a deer fly which had lodged itself in my throat. It had to be the worst bug-infested portage I've ever had to endure.

However, when we returned in September, there wasn't a single insect to be found. It was if we had earned the right to portage into Bolger Lake for the second time without the slightest discomfort.

Bolger Lake has only a scattering of cottages and is not a bad choice for a place to spend your last night en route (the two campsites at the mouth of the southern bay, right of the put-in, are the best on the lake). More secluded campsites can be found, however, if you have time, by continuing east across Bolger Lake, up Bolger Creek. From there, cut across the south end of Portage Bay, portage 937 metres into a small unnamed lake, and then lift over a beaver dam or portage 9 metres into Maple Lake, where you will find three campsites on the north shore. Despite the few developed sections, this entire stretch is rich in wildlife. Great blue herons stalk the weeded bays, ospreys perch high on top of dead snags, and crows swoop from island to island, echoing out their *caws*.

The crow-sized broad-winged hawk, identified by the distinct black and white bands across its tail feathers, also populates the dense mixed woods. In mid-September dozens of these raptors can be spotted soaring high above, waiting to catch a warm air thermal to help them on their long journey to the Amazon rain forests.

A shallow and marshy creek lined by pitcher plants rooted on islands of sphagnum moss takes you north, out of Maple Lake and into a small pond. The Ministry of Natural Resources canoe route booklet has a 177-metre portage marked to the right of the creek. When we paddled through we saw no sign of the trail anywhere. The water level was high at the time, so we had no trouble paddling up the swampy creek and into the small pond.

Directly across from the creek's mouth is the last portage of the trip. A 250-metre path leads you to Wahwashkesh Lake by running alongside a creek on the north side of the bridge, left of the take-out. Near the put-in, submerged debris left from the logging days can be seen on the lake's mucky bottom. The rusted iron and rotten timbers signify the last of the Magnetawan's lumber boom. When the supply of timber dwindled along the Ottawa River and Lake Ontario, the lumber barons moved inland. By the late 1860s the Magnetawan was clogged full of prime pine being driven down to Georgian Bay to be cut in the mills or transported to far-off markets.

Once on Wahwashkesh Lake, paddle east out of the inlet, and then into the northern bay. A grassy narrows on the bay's northeast point will lead you back to the familiar sight of the government dock.

TIME:
3 to 4 days

DIFFICULTY:
Moderate to novice level of experience needed (bring lightweight gear and a Kevlar canoe).

PORTAGES:
14

LONGEST PORTAGE:
2,285 metres

FEE:
The route travels through Crown land and there is no fee required for Canadian citizens.

ALTERNATIVE ACCESS:
The route can be accessed from Highway 69 by way of Naiscoot Lake (the

parking area is west of the highway and on the south shore of Naiscoot Lake), and Harris Lake, east of the highway, 4.6 kilometres along Harris Lake Road.

ALTERNATIVE ROUTES:
Two slightly easier weekend trips can be made by either accessing the campsites on South Magnetawan River by way of Harris Lake or, after organizing a car shuttle, paddling from the Harris Lake access point to the Naiscoot Lake access point.

OUTFITTERS:
White Squall Wilderness Shop

R.R. 1
Nobel, Ontario
P0G 1G0
(705) 342-5324

FOR MORE INFORMATION:
Ministry of Natural Resources
Parry Sound District Office
7 Bay Street
Parry Sound, Ontario
P2A 1S4
(705) 746-4201

MAPS:
The Ministry of Natural Resources has produced a canoe route pamphlet, *Magnetawan River Canoe Route.*

TOPOGRAPHIC MAPS:
41 H/9, 41 H/16

Thanksgiving weekend on the Pickerel River.

7 The Wolf–Pickerel Route

If you're planning to paddle the Wolf and Pickerel River system in midsummer — a route with relatively easy access, few portages, and close to suburbia — expect to contend with crowds of cottagers, boaters and other canoeists. If, however, you pack along an extra sweater and a good supply of turkey jerky, this three-day trip can make an excellent outing for Thanksgiving. Canoeing the last long weekend before winter, spending the crisp days gawking at the splendour of the fall foliage, and huddling by a crackling campfire during the even crisper nights is an excellent send-off for the end of canoeing season.

The route is a horseshoe shape, beginning on the Wolf River and ending on the Pickerel River, and therefore necessitates a short car shuttle. Arrange to have your second (pick-up) vehicle at the federal government dock on Wauquimakog Lake in Port Loring. Turn left off Highway 522 onto Wilson Lake Crescent. The parking area is to the left of Wilson Lake Resort's beach and Jake's Place Diner. To reach the access point on the Wolf River, drive north on 522 just to the point where the highway heads west. Here, continue north along the gravel township road (North Road) for 5.7 kilometres, to where a bridge crosses the river. The parking area is on the far side of the bridge and to the left of the roadway.

The first day is spent paddling the stretch of the Wolf River to Dollars Lake. Along the way the river flows into medium-size Pine Lake and then flows west before entering into Swan Lake. The landscape here is typical of the area, with many exposed, glacier-scoured rocks limiting the vegetation to sparse patches of pine and oak.

A government dam spans the river downstream from Pine Lake. The 130-metre portage marked to the left here is the only portage en route except for a 320-metre path used as a shortcut to the camping areas above Dollars Lake Dam. The second portage can be found near the mouth of the Wolf River, where the river enters the northern tip of Dollars Lake. The take-out is on the western shoreline, directly across from a prominent rock outcrop, and is poorly marked by a single strip of flagging tape. But the last time I travelled the route it took me longer to clamber over the point of land separating the two deep inlets than it would have taken me to paddle around it.

Chances are that you will end your first day early, leaving some time after setting up camp to explore one of the two dam sites. Both sites have walking trails and a place to wet a line. In the past, I've found the fishing much better above the dam and at the mouth of the bay.

From the campsites on the northernmost point of Dollars Lake, the route continues southwest, down the expanse of the lake toward the Highway 522 bridge and Ess Narrows. Just before the bridge, to the left, there is a government dock similar to the one on the Wolf River. This provides an excellent alternative access point if you want to plan a shorter trip.

A 3-kilometre paddle southwest of the bridge takes you to where Dollars Lake meets up with Kawigamog Lake (named after the steamboat that worked the area lakes in the early 1900s). From here the route heads east. The large Crown land islands and scenic rocky points at the eastern end of Kawigamog contain a number of excellent campsites to choose from for your second night out.

At first, Kawigamog, and even the lower end of Dollars Lake, can seem somewhat impersonal, as the lake is constantly buzzed by motorboat traffic. But a canoeist can easily search

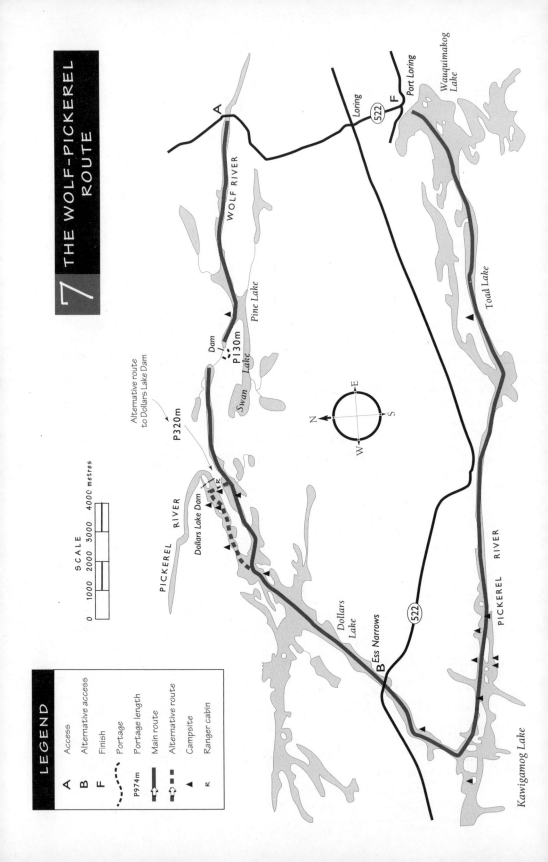

7 THE WOLF-PICKEREL ROUTE

LEGEND

A	Access
B	Alternative access
F	Finish
	Portage
P974m	Portage length
	Main route
	Alternative route
▲	Campsite
R	Ranger cabin

SCALE

0 1000 2000 3000 4000 metres

Alternative route
to Dollars Lake Dam

P320m

P130m

Dam

Swan Lake

Pine Lake

WOLF RIVER

Loring

522

F

Port Loring

Wauquimakog Lake

Toad Lake

PICKEREL RIVER

Dollars Lake Dam

R

Dollars Lake

Ess Narrows

B

522

PICKEREL RIVER

Kawigamog Lake

N E S W

out some seclusion between the islands and rocky channels, and by time evening comes, the sights and sounds of cottage life are lost to the cry of the loon and crackle of the campfire.

The last day of the trip travels east from Kawigamog Lake, up the Pickerel River, to Toad Lake. The 8-kilometre-long river is quite narrow, and its rocky banks are crowned by lush juniper bushes and pine. This diverse forest habitat is a rich area for a variety of bird species, especially the colourful yellow-bellied sapsucker. The woodpecker can be easily identified by its bright red head-patch, a symbol of bravery to the Ojibwa. Legend has it that when the trickster Nanabozho injured himself trying to imitate the bird's tree-pecking, the woodpecker came to his aid and helped stop the bleeding. As a reward for his assistance, the sapsucker was decorated with a dab of Nanabozho's blood.

An early-morning paddle up the Pickerel River is recommended if you wish to view the area's wildlife. By noon the channel is far too crowded with boats and people. And once at Toad Lake, be sure to take the right channel to reach Wauquimakog Lake. The left channel is a 9-kilometre dead end.

All that remains is a 3-kilometre paddle from the outlet of Toad Lake to the town of Port Loring on the northeastern tip of Wauquimakog Lake. Still, this last stretch can be one of the most difficult sections of the route if the winds are up, and especially if you've chosen a cold Thanksgiving weekend for your trip. Just remember, a hot cup of coffee and a slice of pumpkin pie await you at Jake's Diner the moment you arrive at the access point.

TIME:
2 to 3 days

DIFFICULTY:
Apart from the possibility of battling high winds on Dollars, Kawigamog and Wauquimakog Lakes, this is a trip for moderate to novice canoe trippers.

PORTAGES:
1

LONGEST PORTAGE:
180 metres

FEE:
Camping is on Crown land, and a fee is not required if you are a Canadian citizen.

ALTERNATIVE ACCESS:
There is a public access point available on the east side of Ess Narrows,

21 kilometres west of Loring, on Highway 522.

ALTERNATIVE ROUTES:
Canoeists can shorten their trip to two days by accessing Dollars Lake from the Ess Narrows government dock and spending the night on the northern tip of Dollars Lake or on Kawigamog Lake.

OUTFITTERS:
Grundy Lake Supply Post
R.R. 1, Hwy 69 &
Hwy 522
Britt, Ontario
P0G 1A0
(705) 383-2251

When looking for someone to shuttle your vehicle, you will find that there is no outfitter listed

in Port Loring. However, if you visit Buchanan's Hardware or the Esso gas station, you might talk someone on staff into giving you a hand.

FOR MORE INFORMATION:
Ministry of Natural Resources
Parry Sound District
7 Bay Street
Parry Sound, Ontario
P2A 1S4
(705) 746-4201

MAPS:
The Ministry of Natural Resources has produced a canoe route guide, *Wolf & Pickerel River Canoe Routes.*

TOPOGRAPHIC MAPS:
41 H/16, 31 E/13

The calm after the storm (Big Parisien Rapids, French River).

8 The French River
A Historic Waterway

It's the intriguing sense of history that draws me to the French. The moment my paddle dips into the same waterway used by the great voyageurs my imagination runs wild. At times I have even found myself staring out into the river at night, trying to conjure up the flamboyant French Canadians thrusting their red-tipped paddle blades deep into the current. I think every canoeist can feel a kinship with these early explorers while anticipating a trip on the French — not that our modern-day, lightweight Kevlar canoes match up to their 36-foot birchbark canot du maître, but the prospect of adventure is identical.

In 1610, Etienne Brûlé, Champlain's prime scout, became the first European explorer to follow the French River into the expanse of Georgian Bay. Champlain followed Brûlé five years later, and after his exploratory journey, the river quickly became an aquatic highway. Other famed adventurers who paddled the French were the Jesuits, Brebeuf and Lalemant; voyageurs Radisson and Groseilliers; explorer of the western prairies, La Verendrye; MacKenzie, on his way to the Pacific; and Thompson, explorer and mapmaker of the Columbia River.

This historic waterway was designated a provincial park in 1985 and commemorated as a Heritage River one year later. The French River offers more than a rich past; it boasts over 100 kilometres of exceptional canoeing for both novice and experienced modern-day explorers.

The main route paddlers tend to travel is downstream along the entire stretch of the river, from Lake Nippissing to Georgian Bay, a trip that necessitates a lengthy car shuttle. To avoid using two vehicles, however, you can choose one of two loop routes — the Eighteen Mile Island loop on the upper portion of the French, and the figure-eight loop on the lower section, through Georgian Bay.

Route 1: Eighteen Mile Island Loop

The Eighteen Mile Island loop, east of Highway 69, is an excellent five-day trip, providing a chance to practise your tripping skills, particularly the art of lining upstream (guiding the canoe along from shore) and navigating fast-moving whitewater.

Loon's Landing Resort on Dry Pine Bay is where the upstream battle begins. To reach the put-in spot, drive north of the French River bridge on Highway 69 and turn right onto Highway 607. Make a right at the T-intersection, just after the railway, and then take the next left. Keep left on the side road until you reach the lodge on the west shore of Dry Pine Bay.

There are campsites and cabins at Loon's Landing for those who arrive late in the day. Make sure, however, to phone the resort ahead of time (705-857-2175) to be certain of a place to spend the night.

From the put-in, head directly across Dry Pine Bay to Meshaw Falls (formerly Michaud Falls), where you can connect up with Eighteen Mile Bay. Travelling up Stony Rapids, just south of the falls, is an alternative route to Eighteen Mile Bay, but the two portages en route are poorly marked and overgrown. The path around Meshaw Falls, beginning at the private beach of Meshaw Cottages Ltd., is by far the best choice.

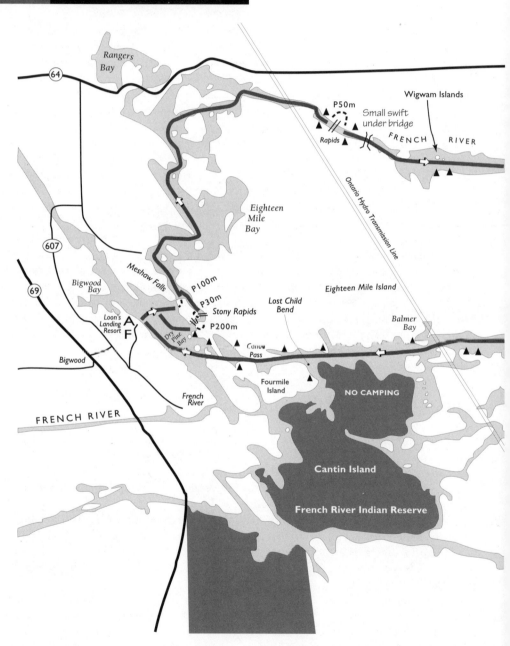

Rangers Bay

64

Wigwam Islands

P50m

Small swift under bridge

Rapids

FRENCH RIVER

Ontario Hydro Transmission Line

Eighteen Mile Bay

607

69

Meshaw Falls

Bigwood Bay

Eighteen Mile Island

P100m

P30m

Stony Rapids

Lost Child Bend

Balmer Bay

Loon's Landing Resort

A
F

Dry Pine Bay

P200m

Canoe Pass

Bigwood

French River

Fourmile Island

NO CAMPING

FRENCH RIVER

Cantin Island

French River Indian Reserve

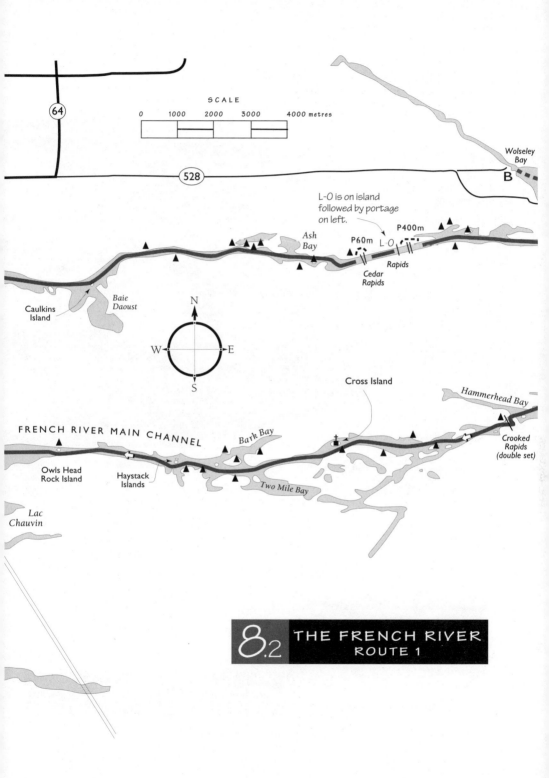

SCALE

0   1000   2000   3000   4000 metres

64

528

Wolseley Bay

B

L-O is on island
followed by portage
on left.

P400m

P60m   L-O
Rapids

Cedar
Rapids

Ash
Bay

Caulkins
Island

Baie
Daoust

N

W   E

S

Cross Island

Hammerhead Bay

FRENCH RIVER MAIN CHANNEL

Bark Bay

Crooked
Rapids
(double set)

Owls Head
Rock Island

Haystack
Islands

Two Mile Bay

Lac
Chauvin

8.2 **THE FRENCH RIVER**
ROUTE 1

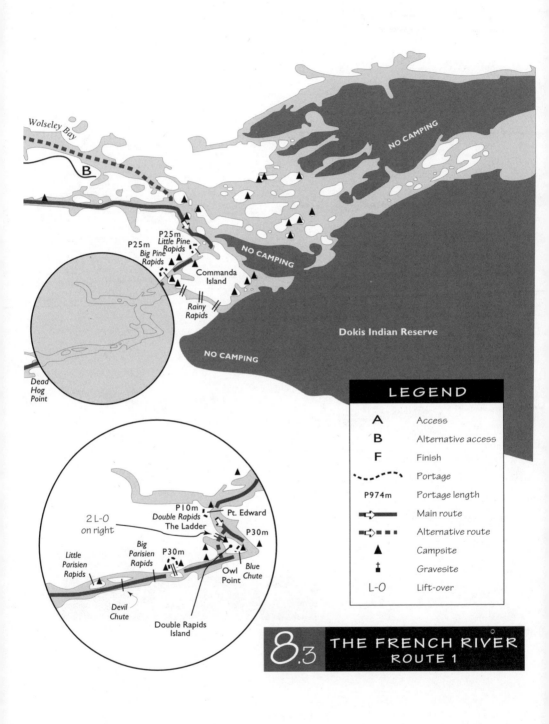

Wolseley Bay

B

NO CAMPING

P25m
Little Pine
Rapids

P25m
Big Pine
Rapids

Commanda
Island

NO CAMPING

Rainy
Rapids

Dokis Indian Reserve

NO CAMPING

Dead
Hog
Point

P10m
Double Rapids
The Ladder

Pt. Edward

2 L-O
on right

P30m

Big
Parisien
Rapids

P30m

Little
Parisien
Rapids

Owl
Point

Blue
Chute

Devil
Chute

Double Rapids
Island

LEGEND

A	Access
B	Alternative access
F	Finish
– – –	Portage
P974m	Portage length
⇨	Main route
⇨	Alternative route
▲	Campsite
✝	Gravesite
L-O	Lift-over

8.3 THE FRENCH RIVER
ROUTE 1

Wolseley Bay, French River.

On the Meshaw Falls portage, up the resort owner's laneway and over a dirt road, take note of a cut-stone wall built around the perimeter of a swirl hole located near the put-in. The natural hole, measuring 1.8 metres across and 4.8 metres deep, was created by the swirling action of a large stone of hard granite. The 68-kilogram stone, which looks something like a bowling ball, is kept on display in the camp's store. .

From Meshaw Falls, paddle the length of Eighteen Mile Bay and then head northeast between the two white quartzite islands. The journey up the French River's North Channel begins here. If luck is on your side, the prevailing winds coming off Georgian Bay will counteract the river's current.

The first rapid along the French's North Channel can be easily lined or waded, though there is a 50-metre portage to the left. Shortly after this point, however, a small swift flows under a metal bridge; you may have to carry your gear up and then back down a steep bank to the opposite side if water levels here are high.

The French opens up after the bridge, looking more like a lake than a river. The first campsite can be found to the south of the Wigwam Islands, at the base of an abrupt granite cliff face. Since most of the North Channel shore is Crown land and is not part of the provincial park (the main channel to the south is part of the park), campsites are not marked or maintained. You should be able to easily find prime sites by searching out well-placed fire rings. If you're still unsure where to make camp, simply ask one of the local cottagers to point out a good site.

I always prefer to bypass the sites south of the Wigwam Islands, paddling past the southern Baie Daoust and Caulkins Island to where the shoreline closes in once again. Here, a few more isolated sites can be found hidden among the hemlock and spruce rooted along the bank, or high atop an exposed bluff, under gnarled and stunted jack pine.

Day two paddling the North Channel offers time out to explore a number of secluded bays and hidden lakes. Abundant bird life (osprey, broad-winged hawks, and even the rare sandhill crane) take refuge in these protected pockets just a stone's throw away from cow pastures and cottage lots.

Only Cedar Rapids (divided into two main sections), halfway to Wolseley Bay, interrupts the river. The first section can be lined or portaged to the left for 60 metres. Farther up the river, the second section, a double set of rapids, requires a little more effort. First you must complete a lift-over on an island in the centre of the rapids. Then you paddle a short distance upstream to where a challenging 400-metre portage is the only way to avoid the final stretch. The trail is found on the left side of the river, running along the top of a ridge. You must first, however, haul your gear up to the top of the rock face, and then search out a series of rock cairns that mark the way.

The second night on the river can be either spent somewhere along the last stretch of the North Channel, where points of pink granite make ideal campsites when the bugs get bad, or on one of the many pine-clad islands dotting the expanse of Wolseley Bay.

The channel receives less motorboat traffic than Wolseley Bay, but if you camp at any of the island sites you can lie in your tent at night listening to the low roar of the nearby Little Pine Rapids and anticipate the next day's downstream run.

The Main Channel runs directly parallel to the North Channel, flushing out of Wolseley Bay in two directions, to the right and left of Crane's Lochaven Wilderness Lodge (first opened for business by the CPR in 1925) on the northern tip of Commanda Island. Little Pine Rapids, the first of seven major rapids known collectively as the Five Mile Rapids, is the preferred route around the island. A 25-metre portage is located in a small bay to the right, but many canoeists choose to either line their canoe down or run straight through the rapid's centre V. There was one trip in late spring, however, when I took the large, curling white waves forming at the base of the rapid for granted and paid the price. The canoe ploughed straight into the foam and froth, bogged itself down with water, and submerged like a submarine. It took two full days before my gear was totally dried out.

The next set of whitewater, Big Pine Rapids, is a little more challenging to run or line, especially where a large boulder juts out three quarters of the way down the run. I have always opted to take the 25-metre portage to the right instead of risking an upset halfway along the trip.

Next comes Double Rapids, which is nothing more than a double swift and can be easily run. Just downstream, however, the river splits, making its way around Double Rapids Island by way of the Ladder to the right and the Blue Chute to the left. The Ladder can be avoided by lifting over the two ledges on the right bank. A steep portage works its way over the centre of Double Rapids Island to bypass the Blue Chute.

The base of the Ladder was the first site chosen by a group of treasure hunters searching the French River for voyageur artifacts in 1961. They speculated that the more turbulent Blue Chute was bypassed by negotiating the large cargo canoes down the twin ledges, and with such a small area to turn between the two ladders, some of the 36-foot vessels may have swamped on the way down. Their hunch was right. The divers swam to the surface with axe heads, brass kettles, glass beads, knives, a musket, flint, balls and shot. After a decade of increased archaeological exploration on the river, the base of the Ladder was one of the two most productive sites on the river for voyageur artifacts.

Downriver from Double Rapids Island the river continues to drop, forming Big Parisien Rapids, Devil Chute, Little Parisien Rapids, and later, west of Hammerhead Bay, a double set called Crooked Rapids. All can be run, except possibly for the unnamed channel preceding Big Parisien Rapids, where water gushes through a narrow slice of the river contained by walls of dull granite. The whitewater here can be avoided completely via the 30-metre portage that follows along the rocky bluff to the right.

Farther downstream, after Big Parisien Rapids, where water levels allow for safer passage over rocky river, it is best to keep to the left to navigate Devil Chute, Little Parisien Rapids and Crooked Rapids.

Beyond Crooked Rapids, the final drop of the staircase ledges, the river loses its white-water, and you will spend the remaining two days paddling a calm and serene strip of water back to Dry Pine Bay.

As the current alters so does the landscape. Gradually the shoreline vegetation changes from forests of stout red and white pine to runty jack pine. Islands with obscure shapes jut out into the centre of the river, each with a story behind its name. Cross Island is said to be the place where a group of Jesuit missionaries in the seventeenth century were massacred, most likely by Iroquois raiding parties from the south on their way to attack the Nippissing band in 1649. Crosses have been erected on the western tip of the island. It's a peaceful spot for a shore lunch, but be warned, the island is still shunned by the local Native inhabitants who consider it cursed. Choosing a place to spend the last night on the river can be difficult. The majority of campsites past Owls Head Rock Island come complete with a massive hydro line humming overhead; no camping is allowed on Cantin Island Indian Reserve; and the sites west of the reserve, along Lost Child Bend (the place where the crying of a lost Native child was heard for six days while searchers hunted the woods to no avail), are ugly as sin. Still, there are a few places to make camp, hidden back in the bay on the north side of Fourmile Island and just west of Canoe Pass, allowing time for a hearty breakfast and leaving you less than an hour's paddle away from the take-out at Loon's Landing the next morning

TIME:
4 to 5 days

DIFFICULTY:
Moderate to novice experience needed in canoe tripping and lining a canoe up and down rapids.

PORTAGES:
13 (depending on water level, most of the rapids along the main channel can be easily run)

LONGEST PORTAGE:
400 metres

FEE:
No camping permit is required for the French River Provincial Park. A small fee is required, however, to park your vehicle at the access point.

ALTERNATIVE ACCESS:
It is possible to start your trip from a number of lodges on Dry Pine Bay or Eighteen Mile Bay. To travel the loop route in reverse, drive east on Highway 64/528 and gain access from the town of Wolseley Bay or Wolseley Bay Lodge.

ALTERNATIVE ROUTES:
You may choose to travel the loop in reverse, beginning and ending at Wolseley Bay, or organize a car shuttle and travel directly downstream on the main channel from Wolseley Bay to Dry Pine Bay.

OUTFITTERS:
Grundy Lake Supply Post
R.R. 1, Hwy 69 &
Hwy 522
Britt, Ontario
P0G 1A0
(705) 383-2251

FOR MORE INFORMATION:
Ministry of Natural Resources
Sudbury District Office
Box 3500, Station A
Sudbury, Ontario
P3A 4S2
(705) 522-7823

MAPS:
Ministry of Natural Resources *French River Provincial Park Canoe Map*

TOPOGRAPHIC MAPS:
41-I/1, 41-I/2

ABOVE: *Portaging couldn't be easier (Bass Creek Tramway, French River).* BELOW: *Canoeists take advantage of the winds coming off Georgian Bay (Main Outlet, French River).*

Route 2: Visiting Georgian Bay

The lower half of the French River, consisting of a figure-eight loop following the historic Main and Eastern Outlets, gives you the opportunity to bless the bow of your canoe out on the great expanse of Georgian Bay. The pilgrimage begins on the docks of Hartley Bay Marina, at the end of Hartley Bay Road. Turn left off Highway 69, just north of the Hungry Bear Restaurant. The put-in can be somewhat crowded, especially on a long weekend, but after you pay for your permit at the main office (located directly across the railway tracks), the marina staff will park your vehicle and help you get on your way quickly.

The route heads west along Hartley Bay for 3 kilometres. Then, upon reaching Turtle Island on Wanapitei Bay, you will turn south toward Georgian Bay.

Wanapitei Bay offers some excellent designated campsites along its western shoreline if you happen to arrive at the access point early in the evening. Be forewarned, however, that all sites along the French River are available on a first-come, first-served basis, and you may find yourself searching for an empty site long after the sun has set and the mosquitoes have come out for an evening snack.

Ox Bay is at Wanapitei Bay's southern end, and it is here where the river branches off into a perplexing array of channels formed by glacial flow and major fault lines. From here the route traces a figure-eight pattern, travelling down the Eastern Outlet to a crossroads called the Elbow, then following the Main Outlet to Georgian Bay, and back up the Eastern Outlet to return to the Main Outlet for the return trip back to Wanapitei Bay. The straight run down the Eastern Outlet, up until a point known as the Whale's Mouth where the channel bends to the east toward the Elbow, provides an excellent view of the Precambrian bedrock of the Canadian Shield. Rocks lie scattered along the sides of the river; some flesh-coloured and ground smooth from the glaciers rolling over them, and others blackened granite, scarred with "chatter marks" created by great mounds of ice and boulders tap-dancing over the bedrock surface millions of years ago.

Hidden behind the scoured shoreline are secluded wetlands where rare plant communities of Virginia chain fern, coltsfoot and nodding trillium can be found. This lush bog habitat is also home to two even rarer species of fauna, the endangered Massasauga rattlesnake, and a small herd of elk, reintroduced to the area in the 1930s.

The first of two portages on this trip is at the Main Outlet's Dalles Rapids, just west of the Elbow. The rapid was an overwhelming surge of water up until 1960 when Ontario Hydro, after being sued for flood damage upriver, blasted islands of rock in the rapid and left behind a pile of jagged debris in the shallow waves.

The take-out of the 180-metre path is on the left bank and is marked by an old boiler abandoned in 1922 when logging activities along the river had all but ceased.

Beyond Dalles Rapids, the Main Outlet heads south toward Georgian Bay, passing by the remains of the French River Village, which was developed by the Ontario Lumber Company in 1875. North of a stunted lighthouse, the foundation of one of the mills is still visible, but most of the buildings (two churches, a post office, hotel and a school) were either torn down for reassembly in Toronto during the 1930s or have rotted away, leaving the French River Village to become another northern ghost town swallowed up by the bush.

At the mouth of the Main Outlet, the river current and the wind from Georgian Bay run at loggerheads, and the battle can undoubtedly create massive whitecaps. But if you time it right, you can paddle out into the oceanlike bay during an evening lull, and make camp on

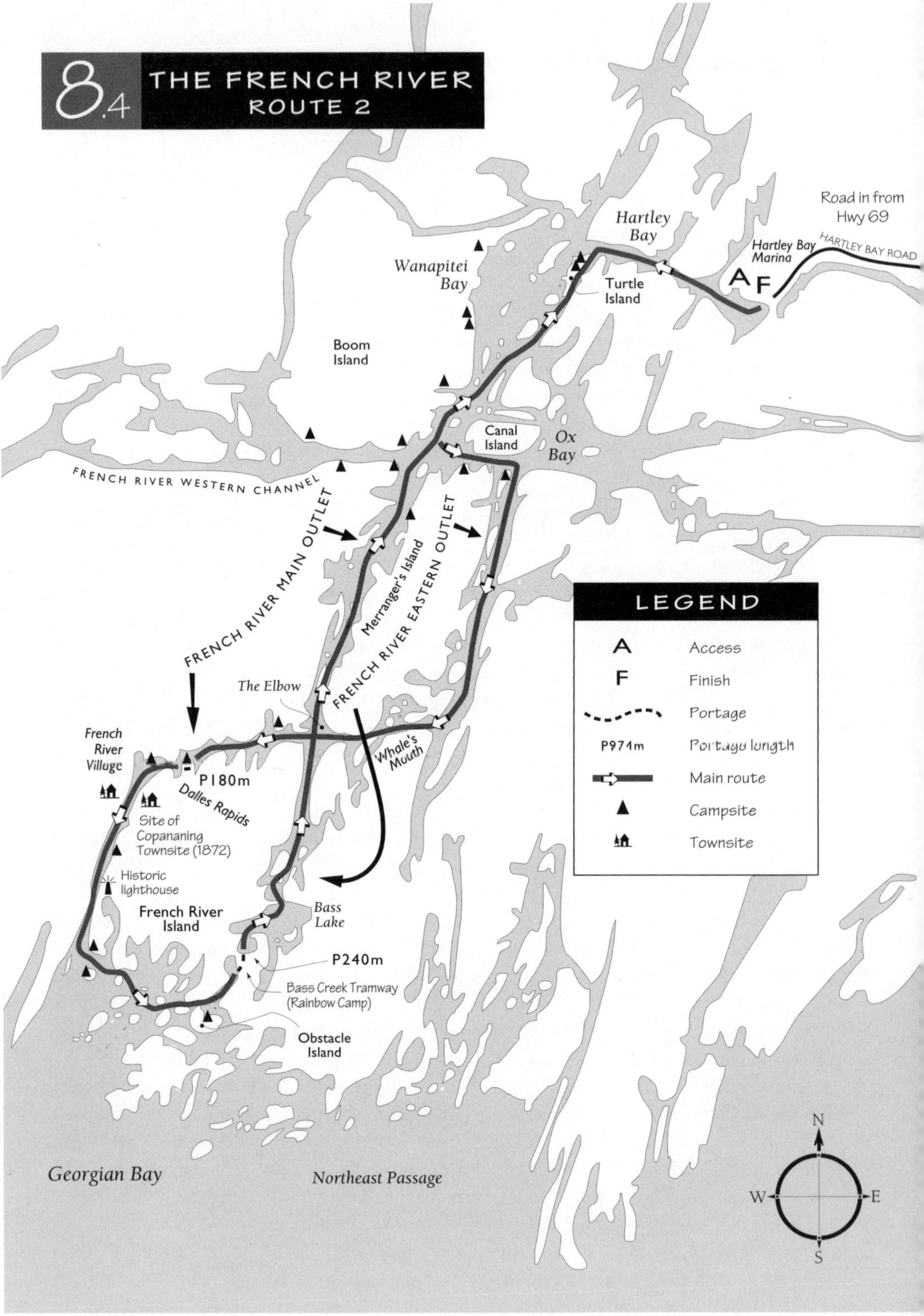

8.4 THE FRENCH RIVER
ROUTE 2

Road in from
Hwy 69

Hartley Bay
Hartley Bay
Marina
HARTLEY BAY ROAD

A F

Turtle
Island

*Wanapitei
Bay*

Boom
Island

Canal
Island

*Ox
Bay*

FRENCH RIVER WESTERN CHANNEL

FRENCH RIVER MAIN OUTLET

Merranger's Island

FRENCH RIVER EASTERN OUTLET

The Elbow

French
River
Village

P180m

Dalles Rapids

*Whale's
Mouth*

Site of
Copananing
Townsite (1872)

*Historic
lighthouse*

French River Island

Bass
Lake

P240m

Bass Creek Tramway
(Rainbow Camp)

Obstacle
Island

Georgian Bay

Northeast Passage

LEGEND

A	Access
F	Finish
⌒⌒	Portage
P971m	Portage length
⇨	Main route
▲	Campsite
⚲	Townsite

N
W — E
S

one of the many rock outcrops or islands crowned with stunted oak and pine. Then come morning, taking advantage of the early calm, you can sneak away and travel back upriver by way of the Eastern Outlet's Bass Creek Tramway.

This 240-metre-long boardwalk, originally constructed of rails mounted on large timbers, was first established as a way for the lumber companies phasing out their operations at French River Village to move their mills elsewhere out on Georgian Bay. The skidway has been rebuilt over the years and used for a number of purposes, from transporting firefighting equipment for the Department of Lands and Forest to providing a shortcut to the Bay for boaters and canoeists. A cluster of cabins at the end of the tramway marks the remains of Rainbow Camp, one of the first of many bustling fishing lodges that operated along the French River in the early 1900s. One of the cabins is left open by the private owner for weary travellers, and comes complete with a weathered logbook for canoeists to sign.

From the put-in at Rainbow Camp, paddle across to the northeastern end of Bass Lake. From there the route continues up the Eastern Outlet, to the familiar intersection with the Main Outlet. Once you've passed the Elbow and are headed up the Main Outlet back toward Wanapitei Bay, finishing off the figure-eight loop, you can either make camp along the channel or catch the prevailing winds with a makeshift sail and leisurely cruise upriver to spend your last night a little closer to the Hartley Bay take-out.

TIME:
3 days

DIFFICULTY:
Apart from dealing with possible high winds out on Georgian Bay, only moderate to novice experience in canoeing is needed.

PORTAGES:
2

LONGEST PORTAGE:
240 metres

FEE:
The French River Provincial Park is an unmaintained waterway park, and no camping permit is required for canoeing the river. However, a fee is charged to park your vehicle at the Hartley Bay Marina.

ALTERNATIVE ACCESS:
French River Supply Post, east of Highway 69

ALTERNATIVE ROUTES:
The route can be extended 2 to 3 days by travelling to Georgian Bay by way of the Western Channel or Pickerel River.

OUTFITTERS:
Grundy Lake Supply Post
R.R. 1, Hwy 69 &
Hwy 522
Britt, Ontario
P0G 1A0
(705) 383-2251

FOR MORE INFORMATION:
Ministry of Natural Resources
Sudbury District Office
Box 3500, Station A
Sudbury, Ontario
P3A 4S2
(705) 522-7823

MAPS:
Ministry of Natural Resources *French River Provincial Park Canoe Map*

TOPOGRAPHIC MAPS:
41 I/2, 41 H/15

George Lake is an excellent place to witness Killarney's drastic geological zone change, where pink granite meets an abrupt protrusion of quartzite.

9 Killarney
Ontario's Crown Jewel

Killarney Provincial Park is truly a paddler's paradise. There's nothing like travelling by way of canoe through the interior's turquoise lakes, surrounded by shimmering quartzite cliffs. And since Killarney is the closest wilderness park to a number of major urban centres, the Ontario Ministry of Natural Resources believes that the park's main contribution to the provincial park system is its role of introducing visitors to their first real taste of a largely undeveloped natural landscape. Killarney is by Ministry definition "a threshold park." To the thousands of visitors who have climbed the quartz cliffs, paddled the turquoise-coloured lakes, and gorged on fresh blueberries from the bushes found in the La Cloche Mountain Range, it is simply "Ontario's crown jewel."

The best canoe route in Killarney's interior is a short paddle to scenic O.S.A. Lake. Originally called Trout Lake, it was renamed after the Ontario Society of Artists (O.S.A.), who, upon the initiative of the Group of Seven's A.Y. Jackson, helped create the provincial park. In 1931, Jackson was headed to Trout Lake on a canoe and sketching expedition when he stopped at Baie Fine to chat with Mr. Spreadborough, a caretaker for the Spanish River Lumber Company. Spreadborough told "Haywire" (his nickname for Jackson) that his employer was planning to log Trout Lake's shores. Jackson could not bear the thought of the lumber company removing the great pines along one of his favourite lakes. So, assisted by friend Fred Brigden and the minister of Lands and Forests, Jackson was able to arrange an exchange of limits with the Spanish River Company, and Trout Lake was saved. The paddle to O.S.A. from the access point at the main campground on George Lake only takes half a day, making it an excellent weekend destination. The problem, however, is that the route is quickly turning into a "hotel wilderness," and it is becoming next to impossible to reserve a campsite on O.S.A. during the summer season. If you find yourself going mad with the constant busy signal on the park's reservation hotline, then have a look at the less-travelled alternative route described at the end of the chapter.

George Lake provides an excellent starting point for visitors who wish to explore the landscape of La Cloche. A drastic geological zone change becomes apparent the moment your canoe rounds the first bend of granite shoreline to your right, revealing an abrupt protrusion of quartzite intermixed with ancient, blackened volcanic sediment.

The first portage, only 50 metres long, is found at George Lake's easternmost end, and there is a wooden dock at the take-out. The second lake, Freeland, is one of the last remaining "living" lakes in the area; water lilies abound here and you'll need to apply extra effort to push your bow through the thick vegetation. Acid rain has killed most of Killarney's lakes, making the turquoise waters as clear and inviting as swimming pools but almost devoid of aquatic plant or animal life.

The portage from Freeland Lake into Killarney Lake to the northeast runs over 430 metres of relatively flat land. The path leads alongside a small stream through a mixed cover of moose maple (mountain maple), birch and pine. Killarney Lake, its surface reflecting the sheer outcrop of white rock, is said to be a mirror image of the landscape near Killarney, Ireland. Loons always welcome you on Killarney Lake. Their mournful cry echoes off the far rocky northern ridge, creating a sense of solitude.

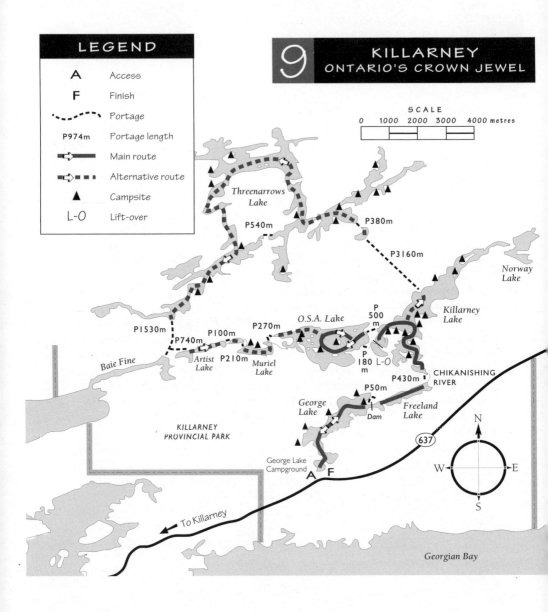

LEGEND

A   Access

F   Finish

· · · · ·   Portage

P974m   Portage length

⬜⮕   Main route

⬜⮕   Alternative route

▲   Campsite

L-O   Lift-over

SCALE

0   1000   2000   3000   4000 metres

Threenarrows Lake

P540m

P380m

P3160m

Norway Lake

O.S.A. Lake

P500 m

Killarney Lake

P270m

P1530m

P740m   P100m

P210m

P180 m   L-O

Baie Fine

Artist Lake

Muriel Lake

CHIKANISHING RIVER

P430m

P50m

George Lake

Dam

Freeland Lake

KILLARNEY PROVINCIAL PARK

637

George Lake Campground

A   F

To Killarney

Georgian Bay

N
W — E
S

Prime lunch stop on First Lake, Spanish River.

ABOVE: The one that didn't get away (Algonquin's Daisy Lake). BELOW: Battling bear-phobia while camped on Missinaibi Lake.

ABOVE: Nap-time (Frontenac's Salmon Lake). BELOW: Whitewater fanatics on Pukaskwa's White River.

ABOVE: Canoeists on Killarney Lake. BELOW: Ridge hiking on Killarney's La Cloche Mountain Range. FACING PAGE: The Barron Canyon, sculptured by melting glacial waters once equivalent to a thousand Niagara Falls.

FACING PAGE: *Cow moose feeding in the shallows of Algonquin's Petewawa River.* ABOVE: *Along the last stretch of the Spanish River the bluffs of rock are taken over by a grassy delta.* BELOW: *Evening light, Lady Evelyn River.*

A fall weekend on the Madawaska River.

"There at last!" Canoeists end the day on Temagami's Wakimika Lake.

Quetico sunset, Batchewaung Bay.

ABOVE: Polished boulders, each with its own unique colour and texture, decorate Lake Superior's shoreline. BELOW: Kerry and Grace investigate a hidden lagoon north of Rhyolite Cove (Lake Superior).

FACING PAGE: Mazinaw Rock, an incredible 100-metre precipice. ABOVE: Making my way up Gull Creek (Mazinaw–Mississippi route). BELOW: White River's Umbata Falls.

*ABOVE: Canoe companion Scott Roberts checking over the map (Daisy Lake, Algonquin).
BELOW: Alana and I camped on Georgian Bay's Sabina Island, located at the mouth of the French River.*

ABOVE: Looking for the perfect tent site (Beatty Cove, Lake Superior). BELOW: Canoeists paddling over the sandy shoals of Lake Temagami's Ferguson Bay.

Big Parisien Rapids, French River.

Island campsite on O.S.A. Lake, with Killarney's Blue Ridge in the background.

O.S.A. Lake is west of Killarney Lake, and can be reached by choosing between a 180-metre portage followed by a lift-over and a small pond, or a lengthy but more direct 500-metre portage through a maple stand where a ghost camp has been swallowed up by thick brush.

Once you set up camp on one of the many islands on O.S.A., you can hike the north ridge for the day or paddle west along Artist Creek and out to Baie Fine on Georgian Bay. There are no set trails heading up the ridgetops; simply choose a spot to park your canoe and commence climbing.

The quartzite ridgetops are spotted with stunted oak (providing excellent habitat for the local deer population), barren rock scarred by lightning strikes, and blackened water pools.

When I reached O.S.A. Lake, I was a bit bewildered by the crowded shoreline, where greenery was hidden by brightly coloured tents, canoe bottoms, and towels flapping on campsite clotheslines. I was lucky enough to find my favourite site open. The last occupants had kindly placed a stack of dried kindling beside the fire pit, and there was a comfortable log situated beside the fire. Everything was set.

I hung my coffee pot over the coals and watched the parade of canoeists as they paddled to nearby islands to make camp for the night: the disappointed fishermen, puzzled to find out that, after coming all this way, the clear lake was completely devoid of fish; the older couple with the yappy poodle who refused to sit still in the canoe; the excited camp kids straining to synchronize their paddle strokes; the teenagers wearing rock-band T-shirts; and finally the college-age lovers who probably couldn't care less where they pitched their tent.

At dusk, O.S.A.'s rush-hour traffic subsided and darkness gradually blackened out the brightly lit campsites cluttering the opposite shore. As night set in, an illusion of wilderness solitude prevailed. Sitting by the water's edge, looking across the lake at my neighbour's campfires as they burned down to glowing embers and then finally died out, I felt the backwoods closing in. The haunting call of a distant loon and the sharpness of the stars shining overhead I'm sure made each of us feel we were alone with nature.

The next morning I watched everybody break camp and pack their canoes for the trip back to George Lake. In just a few hours, the weekend adventure would be over and the reality of the city's daily grind would return. The only thing left would be stories of how rough but enjoyable it was in "the bush."

As I watched the unlucky fishermen, the old couple who were still having problems with Fifi, the exhausted camp kids, the teenagers and the young lovers, I grew increasingly thankful for this not-so-wild wilderness we had shared. Each passing canoeist, who wouldn't have given me the time of day back in civilization, waved a cheery hello and wished me a good morning. Each one of us had different reasons for coming to camp in the heart of the La Cloche interior, but we all had in common a love and respect for the landscape around us.

Before pushing my canoe away from shore, I searched the well-used campsite for any forgotten tent peg, ball of shiny tinfoil or inconspicuous twist-tie. I wanted to keep the camp just the way I found it.

The clear waters of O.S.A. may not be surrounded by hundreds of kilometres of untouched forest, but this beautiful lake and rugged shoreline provide nature enough to satisfy the soul.

TIME:
3 to 4 days

DIFFICULTY:
Moderate to novice tripping experience is needed.

PORTAGES:
3

LONGEST PORTAGE:
430 metres

FEE:
An interior camping permit must be purchased at the George Lake campground for travelling in the maintained provincial park.

ALTERNATIVE ROUTE:
You may extend your trip by two days by taking the long, but relatively flat, 3,160-metre portage as well as a quick 380-metre portage into Threenarrows. To leave Threenarrows loop around to Killarney Lake by way of Artist, Muriel and O.S.A. Lake.

OUTFITTERS:
Killarney Outfitters
Killarney, Ontario
P0M 2A0
(705) 287-2828
(705) 287-2242
(off-season)

FOR MORE INFORMATION:
Killarney Provincial Park
Killarney, Ontario
P0M 2A0
(705) 287-2900
(information)
(705) 287-2800
(reservations)

MAPS:
The Friends of Killarney and Ministry of Natural Resources have produced an excellent map of the park's interior.

TOPOGRAPHIC MAPS:
41-I/3

Alana and I take in the solitude of Killarney's Threenarrows Lake.

Alana scans the cliff face at Ninth Lake for Indian pictographs.

10 The Spanish River

It was mid-June and my wife-to-be and I were in the midst of organizing our upcoming wedding. After dealing with stress-filled days of ordering flowers, booking a dance hall, and mailing out invitations, we decided to escape the premarriage madness and head north for a quick and easy canoe trip. We were in the mood for an adventurous river route with good road access, few portages, moderate level whitewater, and long stretches of unblemished wildlands. With little time to plan, we also needed a route as close to our home in Peterborough as possible. We gave the Ontario road map a quick glance-over and concluded that the Spanish River met our criteria perfectly.

For 142 kilometres the east branch of the Spanish River, beginning at Duke Lake and ending at Agnew Lake, flows through a diverse landscape. One minute you're floating across calm waters, sighting moose and beaver, and the next you're bumping and scraping over sunken gravel bars, riding down chutes, ferrying into powerful eddies, and shooting along strong, deep channels between massive boulders. It's an incredible joyride.

A car shuttle must be organized before you head down the river. Agnew Lake Lodge (705-869-2239) or Stewarts General Store (705-869-3720) is probably your best bet. The roadway in to the lodge is situated just west of Webbwood. Turn right off Highway 17 onto Agnew Lake Lodge Road. The camp is 11 kilometres in from the highway.

For a moderate fee, a driver will drive with you and your vehicle back to Highway 17, then north on Highway 144 until eventually, to the left, you reach a 1.6-kilometre gravel road leading to the northern tip of Duke Lake. Believe me, paying for the shuttle and having your vehicle waiting for you at the end of the trip is far better than driving all the way back to the put-in after spending five days on the river.

The first day and a half of paddling is spent travelling south through a series of ten lakes, numbered in descending order. Each lake is linked by navigable swifts.

I've talked to some canoeists who find this section of the river quite boring and prefer to paddle down the more swift-flowing west branch, from the town of Biscotasing. My opinion differs, however. I find the short swifts help you to practise the whitewater skills necessary for the progressively more difficult rapids waiting downstream. The lake section is also rewardingly pretty and serene. Stands of red and white pine are rooted high atop steep walls of granite, pockets of lowland swamp harbour fragrant meadowsweet, and you can hear the two tributaries (Paudash and Snake) gurgling through lush canopies of birch and aspen before they spill out into the lakes. However, the main attraction en route — a small collection of pictographs painted on a rock face in the northeast corner of Ninth Lake — makes the entire east branch worth paddling. Unfortunately the site has been vandalized by modern-day graffiti, making the pilgrimage somewhat disheartening.

The first major whitewater requiring some attention is Scenic Rapids, between First Lake and Expanse Lake. Supposedly there is a lengthy portage beginning at the south end of First Lake, on the west bank. However, Alana and I saw no sign of the trail on our way through, and decided it would be best to simply manoeuvre carefully down the narrow channel.

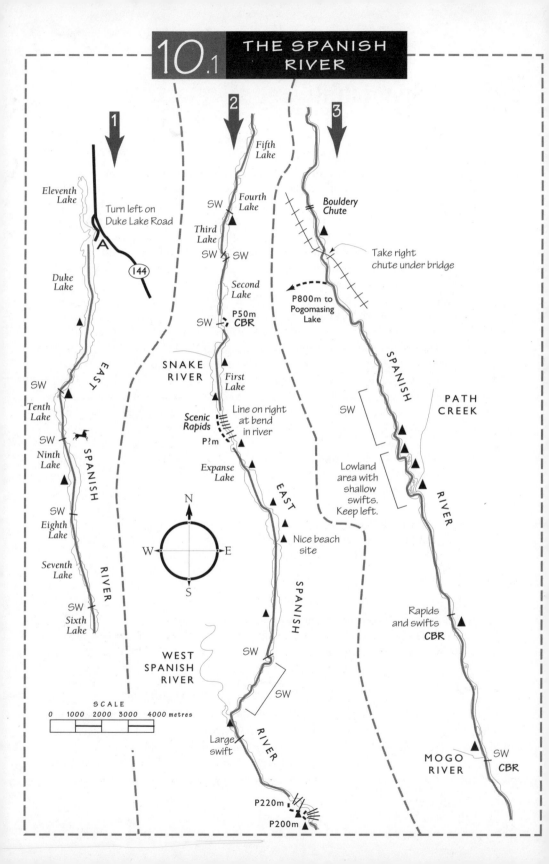

10.1 THE SPANISH RIVER

1

Eleventh Lake

Turn left on Duke Lake Road

A

(144)

Duke Lake

EAST

SW
Tenth Lake

SPANISH

SW
Ninth Lake

SW
Eighth Lake

Seventh Lake

RIVER

SW
Sixth Lake

2

Fifth Lake

SW   *Fourth Lake*

Third Lake

SW   SW

Second Lake

SW   P50m
CBR

SNAKE RIVER   *First Lake*

Line on right at bend in river

Scenic Rapids

P?m

Expanse Lake

EAST

SPANISH

Nice beach site

RIVER

SW

SW

Large swift

WEST SPANISH RIVER

P220m

P200m

3

Bouldery Chute

Take right chute under bridge

P800m to Pogomasing Lake

SPANISH

SW

PATH CREEK

Lowland area with shallow swifts. Keep left.

RIVER

Rapids and swifts
CBR

MOGO RIVER   SW
CBR

SCALE

0   1000   2000   3000   4000 metres

N
W   E
S

4

5

Spanish Lake

SPANISH

P230m

Zig Zag Rapids

AGNES RIVER

WAKONASSIN RIVER

Swift water:
Wide chutes
with obvious
route choices

French Rapids

CBR

CBR
Line to left

P 350 m

RIVER

Cedar Rapids

Nice campsite

Double swift
The Elbow

Eagle Rock

Nice campsite

P100m

Graveyard Rapids

Falls

Agnew Lake

P 150 m

SW

P150m

P500m

SPANISH

RIVER

F

Agnew Lake Lodge

LEGEND

A	Access
F	Finish
- - -	Portage
P974m	Portage length
———	Main route
▲	Campsite
CBR	Check before running
🐎	Pictograph
SW	Swift

AGNEW LAKE LODGE ROAD

17

Webbwood

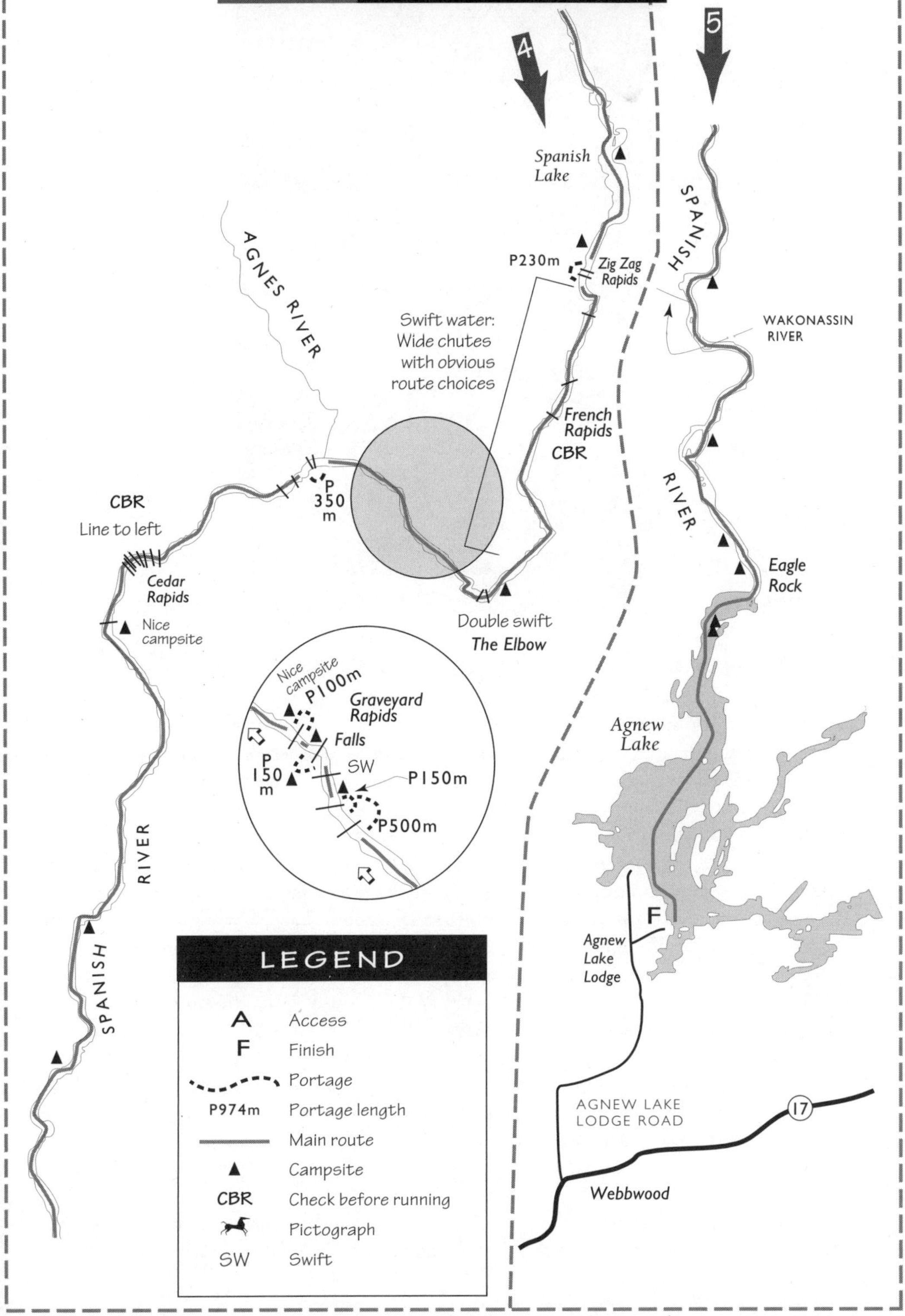

At the put-in at Lain Lake, a plywood sign is evidence of the long-standing struggle for the Teme-Augama Anishnabai to maintain their land claim on Temagami.

What we found dangerous about Scenic Rapids is that it is a very deceptive run. You start off navigating down mere riffles, so mild that it seems inconceivable that dangerous water looms ahead. Luckily, we exited the canoe three quarters of the way down, just before a bend in the river. As we cautiously lined the canoe around the corner, Alana and I beheld three abandoned vessels (a motorboat, an aluminium canoe, and a kayak) wedged into a pile of rocks midstream. We later met the two owners of the canoe downstream, waiting patiently alongside the CPR line to catch a ride on a passing train.

Expanse Lake is a long stretch of open water, and depending on the direction of the wind, it can be either a painstaking paddle or a pleasant sail to get across to the southern end of the lake.

The river speeds up once again at the base of Expanse Lake, starting with a moderate chute, and continues for almost 2 kilometres, gushing over rock ledges and gravel bars right up to the forks where the east branch meets up with the west.

A large island, almost completely covered in thick brush, splits the river midstream. It's best to keep to the right here and paddle between the narrow slice of land and the right-hand shoreline, where the railway track runs along at the top of the steep bank. A 4-kilometre stretch of slow and deep water follows a large swift that must be run shortly after the fork.

The next obstacle is a double set of rapids, one 2 kilometres apart from the other. Both runs have portages (200 metres each) marked to the right. Experienced canoeists usually opt to portage only around the first chute of the first set of rapids and will run the remaining whitewater.

Alana and I made camp at the base of the second rapid, and it would have been a perfect site if it weren't for the brood of blackflies hatching from the deep pools of the river. Just before dusk the mosquitoes joined in the fun, and not being able to stand the hordes of flies any longer, we escaped to the tent. To our horror, however, the teeth of the metal zipper caught on the nylon fabric, leaving a large opening in the doorway for the miniature vampires to find their way in. The bloodthirsty beggars had taken at least a pint of blood from each of us, and just before complete panic set in, Alana ingeniously placed a strip of duct tape over the opening and saved the day. After twenty minutes of swatting the bugs already inside the tent and scratching our even now swollen bites, we dozed off, listening to the insects bounce off the outer walls, sounding something like the spatter of drizzle.

From the preceding rapids to Spanish Lake the river is constantly changing in character, from almost non-existent current to narrow swaths cut through islands of reeds, to ripples of water gliding over gravel lumps, and miniature rapids gushing between high canyon walls.

There are four noteworthy sets of whitewater before Spanish Lake. The first is a bouldery chute that comes shortly after the place where the railway joins the river once again. The second is just downstream, where the river flows under the railway bridge by way of two channels. (As the left channel is too shallow and requires a lift-over, it's best to stay to the right.) The third area is a long stretch of swift water below the ghost town of Pogamasing (Ojibwa for "where water flows over gravel"). The river spreads out over an expanse of sand and gravel bars caused by the Wisconsin Glacier, right up until it spews out into Spanish Lake. Running the rapids is the easy part. Finding the proper channel, however, is quite a challenge, especially just before and after Path Creek. When in doubt, keep to the left of the river. The last section that demands a bit of caution is a rock ledge just after Mogo River. The rapids here may be a little tricky, especially during high water levels.

As the growing river surges sweetly on from Spanish Lake to the Elbow, most sections are simple runs, with wide chutes and obvious route choices. The Zig Zag Rapids, a short paddle down from Spanish Lake, should be treated with some respect. A 230-metre portage is marked to the right, but you may opt to line the canoe instead.

The most serious whitewater on the Spanish, the Graveyard Rapids, is just ahead, approximately 2 kilometres from the Elbow. Here the river valley grows more canyonlike, constricting the current and quickening its pace. A double set of rapids before the main drop can and should be portaged to the right. However, experienced whitewater fanatics can choose to run the first set (watch out for the big, jagged rock midstream), and shorten the 500-metre portage to a mere 150 metres.

After running, lining through or portaging around a short swift between these double rapids and the Graveyard, keep a watchful eye open for the 150-metre portage to the left, which avoids a dangerous falls. Then you must lift over or portage (100 metres) around the next drop along the right-hand shoreline.

Further downstream, vigour renewed, the water cuts a deep bed where the river is pinched narrowly between another section of rock. Here, opposite the mouth of the Agnes River, a 350-metre portage (marked on the left) avoids a short section of whitewater. Two more shallow rapids follow, and these can be easily run or waded. As your canoe floats by, take note of the signs of the river-drive days. Some of the walls of the shantymen's bunkhouses are still visible through the trees, and if you search, you can find pieces of tools scattered about in among the raspberry bushes.

Cedar Rapids concludes the Graveyard series. There is no noticeable portage, and even though the section can be lined along the left bank, it is usually runnable if you carefully check it over beforehand.

The Thunderbird (Ninth Lake, Spanish River).

After Alana and I cautiously lined or portaged the majority of foam and froth upstream, we decided to test our whitewater skills on Cedar Rapids. At the foot of the rapid the current was pulsing under the canoe as we zipped up our life jackets and pressed our knees firmly against the gunwales. Once into the rush of water we were back-paddling vigorously and began shouting our strategy back and forth.

The standing waves played with our boat as we slid downstream, and we braced our paddles on opposite sides to act as outriggers. Then, in the thick of it all, I caught a glimpse of only half a canoe wedged into a pile of dead trees pushed up on shore by the spring flood. A lump formed in my throat.

But after that twenty-second ordeal was over, I suddenly realized how good the boat felt as it responded to our strokes so smoothly, through to the last stretch. Ceremoniously we yelped out a "Yahoo!" and spun our paddles above our heads, and then continued on downstream, relishing every bit of our magnificent teamwork.

As the river twists around a bend, the rapids diminish, leaving only erratic sets of swifts and ripples driving your canoe toward Agnew Lake. Along the last stretch, the bluffs of rock are taken over by a grassy delta. You may catch a glimpse of mergansers paddling downriver in front of your canoe. Listen for the irritable scold of the kingfisher as it flies overhead; the river was originally named after this bird by the Ojibwa.

The only significant rock face is Eagle Rock, at the entrance into Agnew Lake. The granite cliff was believed by the Ojibwa people to be the place where the spiritual messenger of earth and sky, shaped in the form of an eagle, could be found.

I strongly suggest you spend your last night on the river and not at Agnew Lake. The manmade lake was created in 1920 by Inco's Big Eddy hydroelectric plant, and with its eroded banks and flattened landscape, has to be one of the biggest disappointments of the entire route.

Alana and I camped along Agnew's eastern shoreline, where log booms were once anchored between the narrows. Our campsite, near an open field, was a haven for mosquitoes.

We awoke early the next morning, before the insects, and while paddling south down Agnew Lake toward Agnew Lake Lodge, we reminisced about our few days spent on the river. Together we'd paddled across windy lakes, navigated gurgling rapids, and portaged through bug-infested mudholes. Mornings we'd spent cooking up pancakes while waiting for the mist to be burned off the river. And evenings we enjoyed by the dim light of a campfire, going over and over our wedding list, wondering how we could ever gather enough money to wine and dine all of our uncles, aunts, cousins, nieces and nephews.

Four months later, with camp mugs instead of wine glasses placed at the dinner tables, a miniature canoe used as a cake topping, and even guests arriving in animal costumes, our trip down the aisle together went as smoothly as our voyage down the Spanish.

TIME:
5 to 6 days

DIFFICULTY:
Canoeists must have moderate experience in running whitewater (not all sections of whitewater can be portaged).

PORTAGES:
11

LONGEST PORTAGE:
500 metres

FEE:
The route travels through Crown land, where no fee is required for Canadian citizens. A moderate fee is charged to shuttle your vehicle back to Agnew Lake.

ALTERNATIVE ACCESS:
Regular train service from Sudbury will take you to the town of Biscotasing to paddle the West Branch. It is also possible to reach the Elbow from the main highway, although by way of a poorly maintained bush road.

ALTERNATIVE ROUTE:
Rather than paddle the series of lakes on the East Branch, take the train to Biscotasing and paddle the swift water on the West Branch. You can also shorten your trip to three days by organizing a car shuttle to the Elbow through Tom Stewart's Store in Webbwood (705-869-3720).

OUTFITTERS:
Missinaibi Headwaters R.R. 1, Poplar Sideroad Collingwood, Ontario (705) 864-2065 (July & August) (705) 444-7780 (off-season)

Charlton Lake Camp Box 118

Whitefish Falls, Ontario P0P 2H0 (705) 285-4281

for shuttle service Fox Lake Lodge P.O. Box 390 Levack, Ontario P0M 2C0 (705) 965-2701 www.foxlakelodge.com

FOR MORE INFORMATION:
Ministry of Natural Resources Gogama District Office Box 129, Low Avenue Gogama, Ontario P0M 1W0 (705) 894-2000

MAPS:
The Ministry of Natural Resources has produced a canoe route guide, *The Spanish River Route.*

TOPOGRAPHIC MAPS:
41 P/4, 41 P/5, 41 I/5, 41 I/12/ 41 I/13

A quiet evening on Temagami's Obabika Lake.

11 The Temagami Experience

There's no better way to experience the splendour of Temagami than to be taxied by a half-crazed bush pilot to the centre of this wild land and then left behind to find your way back by canoe. After all, it's a tradition among paddlers to have at least one tall tale of a gut-wrenching ride in a Twin Otter to tell around the evening fire.

I'm always up for a ride in a bush plane, so when Wanapitei Outfitters, based in Temagami's Ferguson Bay, invited me along to act as co-leader for one of their eight-day guided packages, I jumped at the chance.

The group consisted of five individuals: Anne; her husband, Pat; his teenage son, Paul; our main guide, Heather; and me. Pat, Paul and Heather took the first flight in, leaving Anne and me to follow with most of the gear. Our pilot, Gerald, shuffled both of us quickly into the cabin of the plane, handed us the packs, lashed a canoe to each pontoon, jumped into the cockpit, and began flipping switches and pulling up levers. Something snapped and the propeller began to turn. Finally, in a mumbled French-Canadian accent, our pilot gave his first command. I leaned closer to ask him to repeat his order and ended up with just a smile. More switches were flipped on and the spiralling prop jolted the plane forward, vibrating the craft until the pontoons finally skipped off the water and we became airborne. Anne and I were obviously in the hands of a genuine professional.

As we flew over the numerous lakes, believed by the Native people to have been created by Gitche Manitou (the Great Spirit) when he threw water from the sea onto the once-parched land, the largest drops becoming Lake Temagami, I pointed out our route to Anne. I'm sure she didn't hear a word I said, but every now and then she would give me a polite grin and then go back to peering out of the plexiglass window to view the breathtaking greenery below.

Twenty minutes later and the plane suddenly dropped out of the sky with its nose pointed toward the sparkling waters of Macpherson Lake. My ears popped and my gut got an attack of butterflies as I spotted the tiny speck of blue Gerald chose to land on. That rushing hiss of water against the pontoons has to be one of the most satisfying sounds in the world.

True to character, our pilot leaped out of the cockpit before the plane came to a full stop. He hastily unloaded the two canoes, our gear, and then us. Before we knew it, Anne and I found ourselves drifting in the middle of the lake, quite bewildered, as Gerald's plane buzzed the treeline and then finally became a tiny dot in the horizon.

We were relieved when Pat, Paul and Heather hailed us from Macpherson's centre island. We paddled over to meet them, and since we had all been in such a rush beforehand, decided to socialize over cheese and crackers before heading out.

After a round of questioning about one another, we began our paddle east, travelling downstream of the Lady Evelyn River — part of the Lady Evelyn Smoothwater Provincial Park established in 1983. Anne and Pat were partners in one canoe, Heather and Paul matched up in the second tandem boat, and I was left to paddle solo.

The Lady Evelyn River, known by the Native people as Majamaygos, "the speckled trout stream," lies on the northern fringe of the Temagami pine belt and flows between mounds of brittle sandstone. To the north is the massive Ishpatina Ridge (the highest point in Ontario); Maple Mountain (the province's second-highest peak) juts out from the rocky landscape to

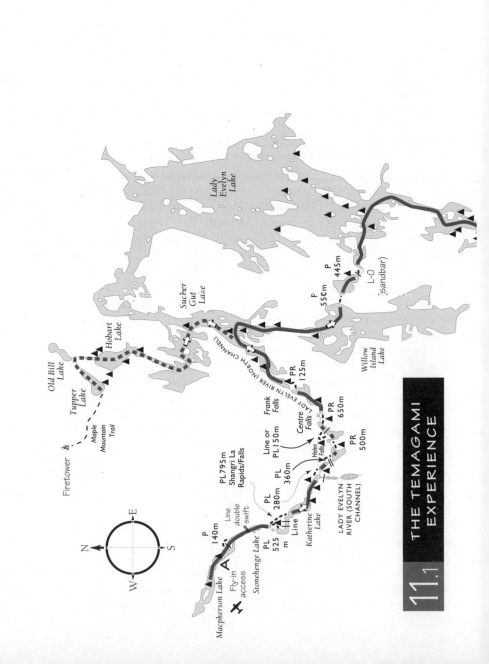

THE TEMAGAMI EXPERIENCE

11.1

Macpherson Lake
Fly-in access

Stonehenge Lake

P 140m
Line double swift

PL 525 m

PL 280m

PL 360m

Line

Katherine Lake

LADY EVELYN RIVER (SOUTH CHANNEL)

PL795m
Shangri La Rapids/Falls

Line or PL150m

Helen Falls

Centre Falls

Frank Falls

PR 500m

PR 650m

PR 125m

LADY EVELYN RIVER (NORTH CHANNEL)

Sucker Gut Lake

Hobart Lake

Old Bill Lake

Tupper Lake

Maple Mountain Trail

Firetower

P 550m

P 445m

L-O (sandbar)

Lady Evelyn Lake

Willow Island Lake

N
E
W
S

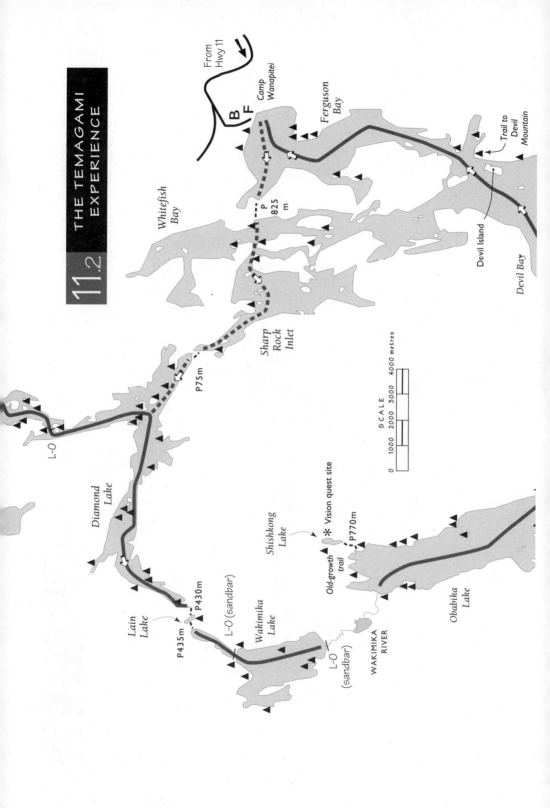

11.2 THE TEMAGAMI EXPERIENCE

From Hwy 11

B
F

Camp Wanapitei

Ferguson Bay

Trail to Devil Mountain

Whitefish Bay

P 825 m

Devil Island

Devil Bay

Sharp Rock Inlet

P75m

L-O

Diamond Lake

Shishkong Lake

Vision quest site

Old-growth trail

P770m

Obabika Lake

Lain Lake

P435m

P430m

L-O (sandbar)

Wakimika Lake

WAKIMIKA RIVER

L-O (sandbar)

SCALE

0   1000   2000   3000   4000 metres

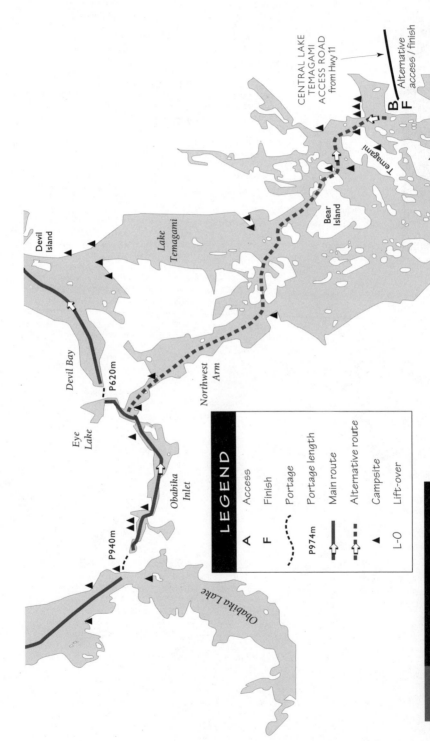

LEGEND

A	Access
F	Finish
	Portage
P974m	Portage length
	Main route
	Alternative route
▲	Campsite
L-O	Lift-over

Devil Island

Devil Bay

P620m

Eye Lake

Obabika Inlet

P940m

Obabika Lake

Lake Temagami

Northwest Arm

Bear Island

Temagami Island

CENTRAL LAKE TEMAGAMI ACCESS ROAD from Hwy 11

B
F
Alternative access / finish

11.3 THE TEMAGAMI EXPERIENCE

the west. The rugged terrain here makes this canoe route suitable only for the sure-footed, especially when rains grease the rocks along the precipitous portages.

The first obstacle en route is a single set of shallow rapids on the north side of Macpherson's second island. Like most of the whitewater on the river, these rockbound rapids are difficult to run, if not impossible. It's best to either take the 140-metre portage (the most level trail on the entire river) marked to the left, or line the canoe down.

Shortly after, two more short sets of whitewater must be lined before you reach Stonehenge Lake — so named for the columns of freestanding rock along its shores.

Shangri La Rapids awaits at the eastern end of Stonehenge. This portage (525 metres) is extremely rugged and begins at the top of a pile of splintered boulders to the left of the river. Along the trail, two secondary paths lead back toward the river to beautiful campsites located alongside Shangri La Falls. Shangri La Rapids, below the falls, can be lined or an extended portage (795 metres) can be used to avoid both the rapids and falls.

After Shangri La Rapids comes Katherine Lake, where at its eastern end the river splits into the North and South Channel. For the North Channel, take the 280-metre portage to the extreme left, followed shortly after by another portage 360 metres in length. Watch your footing at the trail's end. The portage makes its way down a steep slope and ends on a heap of rubble.

However, the most difficult portages still await ahead. Beyond a marshy pond the river's banks narrow as the water is squeezed between walls of gneiss, creating Helen and Centre Falls. Each falls comes with a precarious portage (500 metres and 650 metres) that climbs up and over to the right of the cascades. I'm not sure which of the two is the most difficult. At Helen Falls our group had a tendency go astray if we didn't keep a sharp look out for the odd rock cairn or dull-coloured ribbon tied to a tree to mark the way. But then the short, steep sections along the Centre Falls portage are a complete nightmare. I'm sure that if it weren't for the perfect campsites found halfway along both trails, the Lady Evelyn route would be totally ignored by canoeists.

Between Helen and Centre Falls a short stretch of the river must be waded through or portaged (150 metres) to the left. Our group welcomed the chance to get around the many rocks in the river by wading waist-deep in the water. We had accumulated a considerable layer of dirt and grime on our bodies in just a few days, especially Heather, who had somehow flipped the canoe and fallen into a patch of loon "scat." Boy, did she stink!

One last portage stands in your way between the Lady Evelyn River and the open waters of Sucker Gut Lake. The short but still rugged 125-metre portage is marked along the right bank.

If time permits, plan an extra day to hike up Maple Mountain by way of Hobart and Tupper Lakes. This was a very special place for the Algonquin people. They called the mountain Cheebayjing, "the place where the spirit goes," and believed it to be where the spirits of their dead lingered, watching over the homeland. It takes a few hours to walk up to the summit, but the view from this bald outcrop is supreme.

The shortest way to reach Lady Evelyn Lake from Sucker Gut is to paddle south, into Willow Island Lake, and then take the two portages (550 metres and 445 metres), which connect by way of a small, unnamed lake. Take note that the second of the two portages is well hidden at the far end of the lake, and in low water it may even be necessary to lift over a sandbar just before the trail.

Camping on one of the many scenic islands on Lady Evelyn Lake is a must. The Native inhabitants called the lake Moozkananing, "the haunt of the moose." When explorer Dr.

Bathing beauties taking a dip below Helen Falls.

Robert Bell journeyed through Temagami in 1875, however, he changed the name to honour the sister of the former governor-general, the Marquis of Lorne.

I'll never forget my time spent on this great expanse of water while tripping with Wanapitei. It was around 5 p.m. on day four of our trip when Heather discovered, to her horror, that she had forgotten her life jacket on the previous portage. As I was paddling the solo canoe, I was elected to backtrack while the others found a place to make camp. I paddled against a strong headwind most of the way back to the portage, and it was quite late by the time I found the jacket and returned to Lady Evelyn. My extra hours spent on the water were rewarded, however, when a family of otters swam up to the side of my canoe, slipped under the bow, and then bobbed their heads back up on the other side.

The trip now heads down to Diamond Lake by way of Lady Evelyn's southern inlet, which is cluttered by countless rocky islands. The two lakes are separated by a short lift-over.

Paddle down Diamond Lake's northern arm, and then head west. The lake eventually curves to the southwest, where you will find a twin set of portages (430 metres and 435 metres) heading into Wakimika Lake. The first trail heads across more ankle-twisting Temagami rock to a small pond (Lain Lake). The second trail, marked by a white arrow chalked onto a spread of open bedrock, lies clearly in view on the opposite shore of the pond, so close it seems a burden to paddle there.

At the end of the first portage our group noticed a sheet of plywood bearing this message: "Our land is more valuable than your money. As long as the sun shines and the waters flow clean and pure this land will give life to people and animals. We can not sell the lives of people and animals. We can not sell this land." This was obvious evidence of the long-standing struggle of the Teme-Augama Anishnabai (the Deep Water People) to maintain their land claim. The first full-scale battle occurred in 1972 when the government proposed construction of a year-round resort on Maple Mountain, the spiritual resting place of the local Native people. The Teme-Augama were able to halt the project as well as all development (except for logging) in neighbouring lands encompassing 110 townships. In 1989, however, the court ruled against the outstanding aboriginal land title.

Paddle down the northeast arm of Wakimika Lake and track your canoe over a sandy shoal, and you will come to a historic refuge for another organized group that fought for the preservation of the Temagami wilderness. In September 1989, sixty tents were erected along this kilometre-long beach. The makeshift protest camp was occupied by two hundred environmentalists from across Canada who felt that Temagami's virgin pine, the province's last remaining old-growth forest, should be protected from the logger's chain saw.

The Teme-Augama and the preservation groups, each with separate agendas, have blocked the Red Squirrel and Liskeard logging roads to stop the government from linking them together. The road extension would provide access to the stands of mature pine north of Lake Temagami and south of Lady Evelyn Smoothwater Provincial Park. Even though 150 blockaders have been arrested and 70 charged, the Ontario government still intends to go ahead with the road construction and logging.

There was only a group of loons gathering on the lake in preparation for their journey south for the winter when we arrived on Wakimika. None of us had participated in the protest — the Temagami Wilderness Society called it "the last wild stand" — and when the subject came up around the fire that evening we talked well into the night, debating the rights of nature over the rights of a logger's livelihood. And then, during a brief lull in our heated discussion, a pack of wolves set up a howl from the southeast, where the virgin pine grow out of ancient Precambrian rock. That night camped on Wakimika, as we settled ourselves in the midst of Temagami's "wilderness," we allowed nature to have the last word and quietly drifted off to bed.

From Wakimika's south end, the Wakimika River flushes down into Obabika Lake. The river snakes through dense stands of mixed white pine, cedar, black spruce and birch. Large, submerged tree limbs and old beaver dams clutter the waterway. Most of the brush has been trimmed to make way for a canoe, but once or twice you may be forced to get out and push the boat through.

Three quarters of the way down to Obabika, just beyond where the river opens up into a marshy pond, there is a wooden bridge marked with anti-logging slogans: Tell the rapists go clear cut in hell; Make sure they pay; Spike a tree save a forest. Downstream from the graffiti-covered structure, charcoaled lumber remains of a previous bridge float among the horsetail and sedge grass, cluttering the shoreline, making another strong message against logging in Temagami.

The river eventually opens out into a patch of reeds at the north end of Obabika Lake. Be sure to take the time out to explore the old-growth pine located on the lake's northeastern tip before you begin to paddle the length of this substantial body of water. A campsite atop a rocky outcrop marks the beginning of a trail that leads through the dark, brooding forest and ends up along the shores of Shishkong Lake. For more than 6,000 years, Native peoples have visited Shishkong to complete a spiritual ritual called a vision quest. The belief is that by fasting in solitude for days, one would be granted a guardian angel from the spirit world.

Halfway along Obabika, where the lake narrows, an easy 940-metre portage to the east will take you to Obabika Inlet. The inlet was burned over in 1977, leaving only skeletal

"Lily dippin'" in Temagami.

remains of the forest behind. There is a sense of desolation here. The initial blaze was thought to be under control when firefighters left to work on a more severe burn in Colbalt. The wind, however, took hold of the flaming pine tops and carried the fire across the inlet and to the Northwest Arm of Lake Temagami, burning 10,930 hectares.

The direction you take from Obabika Inlet to Lake Temagami — a lake so big that there is no one point where it can be centrally viewed — depends on where you started your trip. Most flights into the interior take off from the town docks of Temagami at the end of the Northeastern Arm, and canoeists must veer out into Temagami's Northwest Arm from Obabika Inlet and paddle the total width of this 20,210-hectare lake. But since our group's trip was organized out of Camp Wanapitie on the north shore of Ferguson Bay, we headed back to camp by taking the soggy 620-metre portage into Devil's Bay. The trail is located at the far eastern end of Obabika Inlet, along the right-hand side and just before the entrance to weedy Eye Lake.

Steep waves slapped and pitched our canoes dangerously (Lake Temagami is one of the most deadly lakes to be on during high winds), and so the group's paddle on Temagami that day was short-lived. We quickly drifted into a protective bay close to the base of Devil Mountain and nearby Devil Island. Both landforms, formed, geologically speaking, by the intrusion of the Nippissing Diabase, have a noteworthy history. Native legend has it that an evil spirit, Matche Manitou, came to live on Devil Island to plague the Algonquin people with the scourge of the blackfly. He then later moved to the jagged cliffs of Devil Mountain, and it was here that the people attempted to appease the spirit by giving Matche Manitou a wife, called Kokomis (grandmother). The woman, however, was unable to change the spirit's evil ways, and after a quarrel with him she fled into the lake. Matche Manitou became furious with Kokomis and from the cliff he threw four chunks of rock down at her. The woman dragged herself to shore on a fifth, larger rock before Matche Manitou finally turned the "grandmother" to stone. The five islands can be seen south of Devil Island; a small rock on the main Granny Island resembles a woman with her head resting between her hands.

A steep trail up to Devil Mountain's summit begins from a perfect campsite on the main shore just past the northern tip of Devil Island. The last night of our trip was a memorable one. After a glowing sunset the skies clouded and a light rain began to fall. We all snuggled together under a leaky tarp, sharing a pot of tea and reminiscing over our week spent in the wilds of Temagami. Each of Wanapitei's customers summed up the trip in a simple statement. Pat, remembering back to the slick portages along the Lady Evelyn River and harsh winds on Obabika Lake, joked, "I could have saved myself the price of a Tilley hat and stayed home to slash my wrist with a dull kitchen knife, and got the same result." Paul quickly replied, "Ah, come on, Dad. It was a lot of hard work, but I'd do it again in a second!" And Anne ended with a much more solemn note. "When you're out here, this is everything that is real; all the rest of the world's worries are long forgotten. And that's what you want in a vacation."

The next morning the weather was still foul and it seemed we were destined to end the trip hammered by wind and waves while we paddled north to Ferguson Bay. However, by the time we pulled the canoes up on the sandy beach to the left of Camp Wanapitei and carried our gear up the trail to the designated parking area, the skies had cleared and the sun beamed down upon us. We ended our "Temagami experience" with a group hug and planned a sequel to our adventure before driving back toward Highway 11 along the dusty Red Squirrel Road.

TIME:
6 to 8 days

DIFFICULTY:
Only a moderate level of canoeing experience is needed. However, canoeists must be physically fit due to extremely rugged portages along the Lady Evelyn River and high winds on Lady Evelyn, Diamond, Obabika and Temagami Lakes.

PORTAGES:
15

LONGEST PORTAGE:
An easy 940 metres, but it does not compare to the 500 metres and 650 metres around Helen and Centre Falls on the Lady Evelyn River.

FEE:
No permit is needed for canoeing through Lady Evelyn Smoothwater Provincial Park. The rest of the route travels through Crown land, where Canadian citizens do not require a camping permit. Expect to pay a moderate fee, however, if you plan to fly in.

ALTERNATIVE ACCESS:
You can begin at the town docks in Temagami, or turn left off Highway 11 just before the town and take the Lake Temagami Access Road all the way to the mouth of the Northeast Arm.

ALTERNATIVE ROUTES:
If you don't want to fly in, park your vehicle at the Temagami town docks, the end of the Lake Temagami Access Road, or the parking area near Camp Wanapitei on Ferguson Bay. From any of these points an excellent loop route can be had by way of Lake Temagami's North Arm, to Sharp Rock Inlet, Diamond Lake, Wakimika Lake, Wakimika River, and Obabika Lake, and back to Lake Temagami. This route avoids the rugged Lady Evelyn River.

OUTFITTERS:
Lakeland Airways
Box 249
Temagami, Ontario
P0H 2H0
(705) 569-3455

Wanapitei Wilderness Centre
393 Water Street, Suite 14
Peterborough, Ontario
K9H 3L7
(705) 745-8314

Smoothwater Outdoor Centre
Box 40
Temagami, Ontario
P0H 2H0
(705) 569-3539

Temagami Wilderness Centre Limited
R.R. 1
Temagami, Ontario
P0H 2H0
(705) 569-3733

Temagami Outfitting Company
Box 27
Temagami, Ontario
P0H 2H0
(705) 569-2790

FOR MORE INFORMATION:
Ontario Ministry of Natural Resources
Temagami District
Box 38, Lakeshore Drive
Temagami, Ontario
P0H 2H0
(705) 569-3622

TOPOGRAPHIC MAPS:
41 P/1, 41 P/8, 41 I/16

"Good to the last drop" (White River).

12 White River to Lake Superior

It was the simple idea of paddling downriver to the legendary waters of Lake Superior — the world's largest freshwater inland sea — that first interested me in canoeing the White River. But the moment my topographic maps came in the mail and I unrolled them out on the kitchen table to catch the first glimpse of the snakelike strip of blue running across the paper, with its dark brown contour lines indicating the countless rapids and falls along the way, I knew the White would become one of the toughest, most dangerous, and magnificent canoe trips of my life.

Considering the river's rugged terrain and seemingly remote setting, I opted out of a solo excursion and asked a few friends I knew from the college I lecture at during the winter months to tag along. Al McPherson and Neil Steffler, both instructors in the Parks and Recreation Department, partnered up in one canoe. And joining me in my canoe was John Buck, the now retired associate dean, who, with his grey beard and weathered Tilley hat pulled down past his ears, reminded me more of a present-day version of Canada's canoe guru Bill Mason than a college administrator.

The route begins at White Lake Provincial Park, which is located along the Trans-Canada Highway (Highway 17), 35 kilometres west of the town of White Lake and 72 kilometres east of Marathon.

The park staff will register you for travelling through White Lake Provincial Park and then inform you how to obtain a permit for Pukaskwa National Park, and will also provide someone to shuttle your vehicle to the national park's visitor centre parking lot in Hattie Cove. You can register at either the main gate or the registration booth down at the provincial park's launching site.

The Native people call the lake Natamasagami, meaning "first lake from Lake Superior." It was the European voyageurs and traders who, having to constantly battle the whitecapped waves whipped up on the northern end of the lake by heavy winds, gave it its present name. The section of the lake you will be travelling on is quite sheltered, however.

Travel in a southwesterly direction and you will eventually paddle under a railway trestle and then to the Ministry of Natural Resources dam. This is where water levels are controlled, allowing the White River to be accessible throughout the entire paddling season.

The first portage en route is right of the dam (240 metres). During the summer season, you can usually shorten the portage to 65 metres by lifting your gear and canoe up and over on the right of the metal structure, and then navigating the swift water down below.

Shortly after the dam, a series of rapids mark where the river begins to drop down off the Canadian Shield. These rapids can be bypassed by four portages. The first, a long 575 metres, is marked to the left. Along the path, however, you will notice a trail breaking off the main portage and working its way back to the river. This is where experienced whitewater canoeists have shortened the carry by navigating some of the runnable sections between the two major drops.

Along the entire route you'll notice a number of side trails on the portages. To keep it simple I have decided to only include the main portages en route, leaving you to judge your own experience level while scouting out each run.

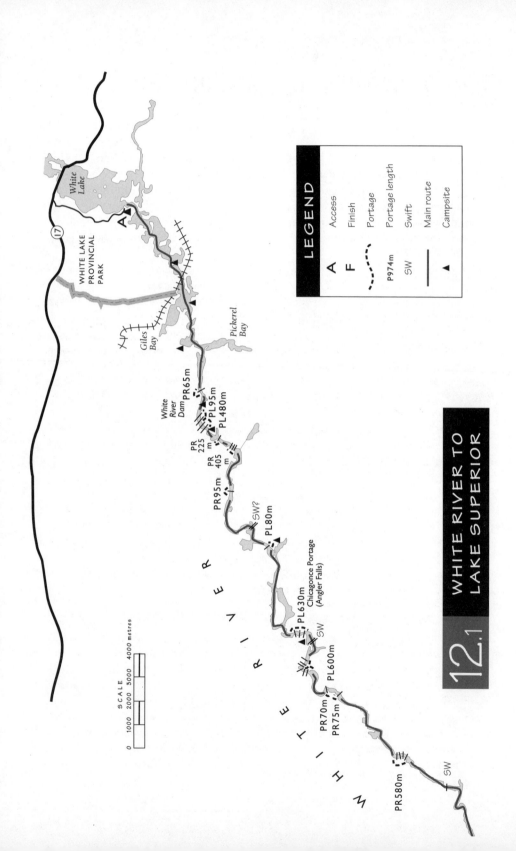

LEGEND

A   Access
F   Finish
    Portage
P974m   Portage length
SW   Swift
    Main route
▲   Campsite

12.1   WHITE RIVER TO LAKE SUPERIOR

White Lake

17

WHITE LAKE PROVINCIAL PARK

Giles Bay

White River Dam

Pickerel Bay

PR65m
PL95m
PL480m
PR 225 m
PR 405 m
PR95m
SW?
PL80m
Chicagonce Portage (Angler Falls)
PL630m
SW
PL600m
PR70m
PR75m
PR580m
SW

W H I T E   R I V E R

SCALE
0   1000   2000   3000   4000 metres

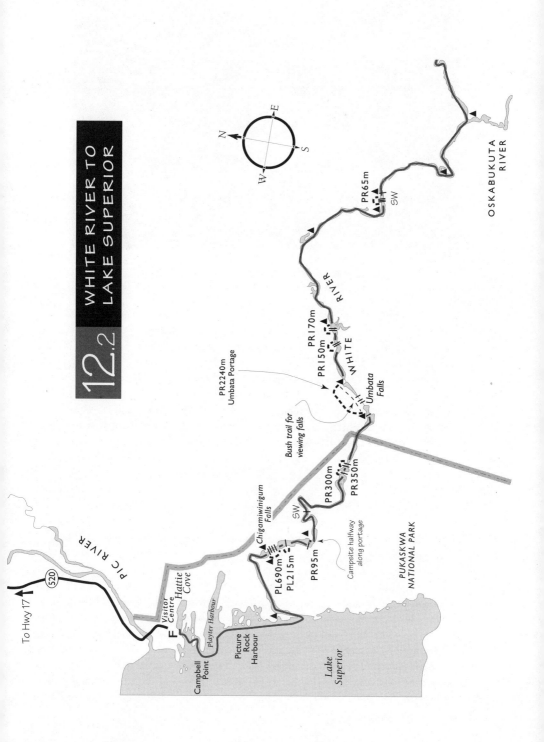

12.2 WHITE RIVER TO LAKE SUPERIOR

To Hwy 17

520

PIC RIVER

Visitor Centre

Campbell Point

Player Harbour

Hattie Cove

Picture Rock Harbour

Lake Superior

PL690m

PL215m

Chigamiwinigum Falls

SW

PR95m

Campsite halfway along portage

PR300m

PR350m

PUKASKWA NATIONAL PARK

Bush trail for viewing falls

PR2240m Umbata Portage

Umbata Falls

PR150m

PR170m

WHITE RIVER

PR65m

SW

OSKABUKUTA RIVER

N
E
S
W

A wooden cross marks the site where kayaker Jerry Cesar plunged to his death at Angler Falls (White River).

Downstream there is a 225-metre portage to the right, followed soon after by a 405-metre portage with a steep take-out just before a sharp bend in the river, and then a 95-metre portage also to the right.

For 4 kilometres the river slows down and is free of any portages. If you check the older maps, however, a path is marked around the first bend. The strange thing is that not even the slightest ripple exists here, let alone a major rapid. Instead, the river is calm and incredibly deep. It's been said that the portage was cleared by travelling Ojibwa years ago. They called it the land of Misshepezhieu, and chose to portage around this section of the river because they believed it was home to a dragonlike monster who dwelled at the bottom of the river, waiting to overturn canoeists who paddled by. To ensure yourself safe passage it might be wise to toss a bundle of sacrificial tobacco over the gunwales to appease the mythical creature.

Our party, laden with superstition, quickened the pace through the site and made camp further downstream at the end of an 80-metre portage marked on the left of a stunted rapid. The site would have been perfect for our first night on the river if not for a noisy skidder, busy dragging spruce and jack pine logs through the bush not even 500 metres from our tents. Florescent flagging tape, wrapped around a line of cedar trees, had also been left by mine claimers in search of the Hemlo gold motherlode.

Both the logging and mining companies had legal permits for their work in the area, but the drone of machinery and swaths of surveying tape, plus the rumour we heard before heading out on the river that Ontario Hydro plans to develop three dams along the river's length, quickly dissolved any notions we had of enjoying a wilderness experience the first day out on the river.

Early the next morning, before the loggers started up their chain saws, we packed up and escaped downriver, where the low-lying banks of cedar, poplar and birch are replaced by steep knolls topped with pinhead-shaped spruce. Here, the river takes another dramatic tumble off the Shield at Angler Falls.

John and I could hear the low, unmistakable roar of the waterfalls seconds before we nosed our canoe around a bend in the river. The banks quickly closed in and a small swift was formed ahead of the brink of the cascade, where the entire river flushed through and left only a fine mist floating skyward.

For a brief second, John and I pondered the idea of lining the canoe through the swift to cut some length off the 630-metre portage running along the left bank. As we caught sight of a wooden cross, erected years ago by the partner of a kayaker who drowned at this spot, we quickly made our decision and beached the canoe right at the marked take-out point.

Before carrying over the portage, we took a close look at the cross, which read, "Jerry Cesar / Born 11-26-40 / Drowned here 5-17-75 / Always at home in the bush / Now at home in Heaven / He believed in Jesus Christ."

The story is that the kayaker paddled around the bend in the river and was surprised by the surge of high flood waters. The quickened current overtook him, and he grabbed blindly for a low-hanging branch near the brink, but it snapped. The kayak was recovered, but the paddler's body has never been found.

From the steep put-in at the base of Angler Falls, you must navigate a quick swift before unloading your canoe once again, to portage a total of 600 metres along the left bank.

After a brief paddle, two short portages (70 metres and 75 metres) are marked on the right. The first avoids a runnable swift. The second, however, must be used to work around a maze of ledge rock and bellowing whitewater.

The next obstacle, a stunted falls, has a 580-metre portage to the right with an excellent sandy campsite at the put-in.

It was here that our uneventful voyage down the White took a turn for the worse. Clear skies quickly blackened without warning and torrential rain soaked us to the skin. Feeling miserable from the surprise downpour, we decided to erect camp on the sandy point at the end of the portage, and to help boost our morale, I opened a can of oysters to snack on before dinner. Little did we know that each slimy marine mollusk we swallowed was toxic. Neil was the first to feel the ill effects of severe food poisoning, and as the trip progressed, so did the group's acute gastrointestinal condition. To make matters worse, the rain continued throughout the next few days, soaking every roll of toilet paper we had, except for one. By working together as a team, however, we pulled through the hellish ordeal and we were even able to enjoy the rest of the trip.

Between the last set of rapids and Umbata Falls (a distance of approximately 25 kilometres) the course of the river is somewhat uneventful except for a few swifts before and after where the Oskabukuta River meets up with the White, and two sets of rapids just ahead of the falls. Both sets have portages (170 metres and 150 metres) marked to the right that make use of the Umbata Road, which runs parallel to the river.

Umbata Falls is awe-inspiring. We could hear the muted rumble of water plunging downhill from at least 2 kilometres away. As you approach the monstrous cascade, the current seems to slacken, as though the water was resting up before it gathered force and then leaped down into the gorge below. Our group found ourselves inching our canoes along the north side of the river well before the take-out, fear building as the void drew nearer.

The Umbata Falls portage, measuring 2,240 metres in length, begins at a very steep embankment and then follows the Umbata Road. Near its end, the road comes to a hydro line and heads back down to the river. The put-in is 100 metres downstream from where a bridge crosses the White. Two side trails can be taken on the north side of the river to view the spectacular 100-metre drop. The first is near the beginning of the portage and the second is at the base of the falls (200 metres upstream of the bridge), to the left of a patch of alders.

Pukaskwa National Park is just below Umbata Falls, and it seemed that the moment we passed the government sign indicating the border of the federal park, wildlife became more abundant: curious grey jays perched themselves on tops of spruce trees to watch us drift by; sandpipers fluttered from rock to rock along the banks; a bald eagle soared high overhead; and even a moose made a rare appearance.

The landscape grows more rugged here, and as the high rocky banks thick with coniferous forest closed in, it seemed each turn in the river revealed another cascade.

A total of five falls can be counted in Pukuskwa before the White drains into Lake Superior. The first three are avoided by portages on the right bank (350 metres, 300 metres and 95 metres). Each of these portages is extremely steep and rugged, with piles of driftwood cluttering up every put-in.

The two final sets of falls are portaged on the left bank (215 metres and 690 metres), where the Pukaskwa Coastal Hiking Trail runs parallel to the river. Be aware that at the take-out of the last portage there are three trails branching out in different directions. The portage (named Chigamiwinigum Portage) heads directly up the hill, but it's worth your while to take time out to follow the hiking trail to the right. The path leads to a footbridge that crosses a deep-cut gorge in the river.

Less than an hour's paddle from Chigamiwinigum Portage, the White River drains into the expanse of Lake Superior.

When our group paddled out the mouth of the White, it seemed as if we had passed through a gateway into some type of dream world. The lake, notorious for its deadly wind and waves, was as smooth as a duck pond. The sky, however, was marked with an assortment of cloud formations: stratus, nimbostratus, and cumulonimbus — all of which indicate an approaching thunderstorm. The paddle up along the coast to Hattie Cove takes approximately two hours, and we were forced to decide whether to take advantage of the calm before the storm or wait and hope that the lake would be smooth again the next day. Experience told us that the likelihood of having two calm days in a row out on Lake Superior was minimal — not to mention that the idea of spending another night in the bush while fighting the ill effects of toxic oysters was unthinkable — so we voted to tempt our luck, and headed north.

For the first hour things went relatively well; we stuck close to shore, back behind the islands of Picture Rock Harbour. Then we reached the southern lip of Playter Harbour, where we were forced to cut across the width of the inlet to Campbell Point, a sheer wall of granite where beaching a canoe would be literally impossible. By looking at the topographic map, however, we figured that once we rounded the rocky point we would be safe among the islands of Pulpwood Harbour, just south of the entrance to Hattie Cove.

Ten minutes after breaking away from Picture Rock Harbour our canoes began fighting a slight choppiness — not much, but enough to give us a sense of our vulnerability. We began paddling harder. There were no lackadaisical strokes; we dug our paddle blades deep into the frigid waters for maximum effect. Campbell Point was really quite close, but to us, wrapped up in a state of near panic, it seemed to hang in the distance like a desert mirage.

By the time we rounded Campbell Point all our energy had been drawn, and we were forced to stop paddling between the rock cliff and the islands of Pulpwood Harbour. But as we drifted offshore, a thick fog dropped down — a reminder that the lake was still in full control of our destinies.

As the murky vapour cloaked everything around us, the group's whereabouts became dependent on my compass skills. Twenty minutes of paddling and a bearing of 56 degrees lead us to the sandy beach of Hattie Cove Campground, seconds before a fresh breeze blew in a major storm front that lasted three full days.

We were safe! Looking back to the perils of previous trips — a bear encounter on the Missinaibi River, almost swamping at the foot of Graveyard Rapids on the Spanish, weathering out hurricane winds under a collapsed tent on Algonquin's Big Trout Lake — I can say that paddling Lake Superior just ahead of an approaching storm was the only time I felt my life was in jeopardy. The idea of being tossed into the deadly cold water and then bashed against sheer rock was truly frightening. In retrospect I've come to realize that my good fortune was not that my skills as a canoeist got me to Hattie Cove, but rather that the spirits of this freshwater inland sea allowed me to survive that day.

TIME:
5 to 7 days (count on at least one day windbound on Lake Superior)

DIFFICULTY:
Even though most rapids and all cascades are equipped with portages, the route is extremely demanding physically, and a high level of experience in river tripping, moderate whitewater skills, and a large degree of awareness of the dangers of river currents and high winds out on Lake Superior are needed.

PORTAGES:
20

LONGEST PORTAGE:
2,240-metre portage around Umbata Falls

FEE:
An interior permit must be purchased at the gate of White Lake Provincial Park for travelling through Pukaskwa National Park. Upon completion of your trip you must sign out at the park visitor centre in Hattie Cove or at the registration booth at the mouth of the Pic River.

ALTERNATIVE ACCESS:
You can start from Negwazu Lake, located east of Highway 17, reached by way of a dirt road from Obatanga Provincial Park.

ALTERNATIVE ROUTES:
If you're interested in canoeing the entire river you can begin at Negwazu Lake. Highway 17 and the Canadian Pacific Railway (CPR) also cross the river at several points. For information on the CPR, contact VIA Rail, 20 King Street, Toronto, Ontario M5H 1C4 (1-800-361-1235). It's important to note, however, that water levels on the upper section of the river, before White Lake, can be extremely low, and at the present time it is poorly maintained by the Ministry of Natural Resources.

OUTFITTERS:
Boat Charter Services for pickup on Lake Superior:
K.T. McCuaig & Sons Ltd.
Heron Bay, Ontario
POT 1RO
(807) 229-0605 (office)
(807) 229-0259 (home)
Naturally Superior Adventures
RR#1 Lake Superior
Wawa, Ontario
P0S 1K0
(705) 856-2939

FOR MORE INFORMATION:
Ontario Ministry of Natural Resources
(705) 856-2396
Pukaskwa National Park
(807) 229-0801
White Lake Provincial Park
(807) 822-2447

MAPS:
The Ministry of Natural Resources has produced a canoe route pamphlet covering the entire river, *White River Canoe Route*.

TOPOGRAPHIC MAPS:
Marathon 42 D/9, Cedar Lake 42 C/12

The rock at Missinaibi Lake's Fairy Point is adorned with over a hundred Native pictographs.

13 The Magic of the Upper Missinaibi

During my college years in Sault Ste. Marie I spent many weekends chumming around with Jim Black, a fellow student. We were notorious for cutting class early on Friday and driving north to visit Jim's grandfather, who lived on the reserve just west of Wawa.

Much of our time was spent roaming the bush on foot, helping Jim's grandfather check his trap line. However, there were those special occasions when the grandfather would tie his old cedar-strip canoe on top of Jim's rusted-out pickup and take us somewhere for a paddle.

One memorable trip was on the Michipicoten River. We left the screaming gulls of Lake Superior behind and headed upstream, battling a continually changing current caused by a series of hydroelectric dams obstructing the Michipicoten's flow. It seemed that we spent more time portaging around cement structures and passing under humming hydro lines than soaking up the wilds of the waterway.

We made camp overnight on the river, and Jim's grandfather told us countless stories of his travels up the Michipicoten to visit the Missinaibi River, a place where he believed the land still remained wild and the spirits could still flow free.

The next morning, before we packed up and headed back down to Lake Superior, I made a promise to Jim's grandfather to return one day to paddle the river he spoke of the night before. And for ten days in July, eight years later, I took a solo pilgrimage in search of the spirits of the Missinaibi.

It still is possible for a canoeist to travel right from Lake Superior by way of the Michipicoten River, and then down the entire length of the Missinaibi and Moose Rivers to the salty waters of James Bay. However, most canoeists only have time to paddle either the upper section (236 kilometres), from the town of Missanabie to Mattice, or the lower section (316 kilometres), from Mattice to Moosonee.

I had an ongoing debate with my canoeing cronies before I left on my solo trip on what was the best section of river to travel. Many canoeists said that they would choose to paddle the lower section so as to view the incredibly scenic Thunderhouse Falls and to be able to bless the bow of their canoe in the Arctic waters of James Bay. Other paddlers preferred the upper section for its more technically challenging rapids.

It was the upper section I chose, and not out of a desire to playboat in whitewater, but for a more practical reason; the upper section of the Missinaibi happens to be far easier and cheaper to access than the lower.

Of course, like any other great river canoe route, the upper Missinaibi still requires a lengthy car shuttle. To allow more time spent paddling on the river, I opted to pay Missinaibi Outfitters (call 705-364-7312 in summer) to store my vehicle while I was on the river and then have it waiting for me at the take-out spot in the town of Mattice on my scheduled arrival date.

After considering the countless places to begin the trip on the upper Missinaibi (see the alternative route information given at the end of the chapter), I found the best access point that met my needs was beside the hotel in the village of Missanabie. The hotel is on the far side of town, near Dog Lake. To reach the small hamlet, drive to the end of Highway 651, approximately 50 kilometres north of Highway 101.

13.1 THE MAGIC OF THE UPPER MISSINAIBI

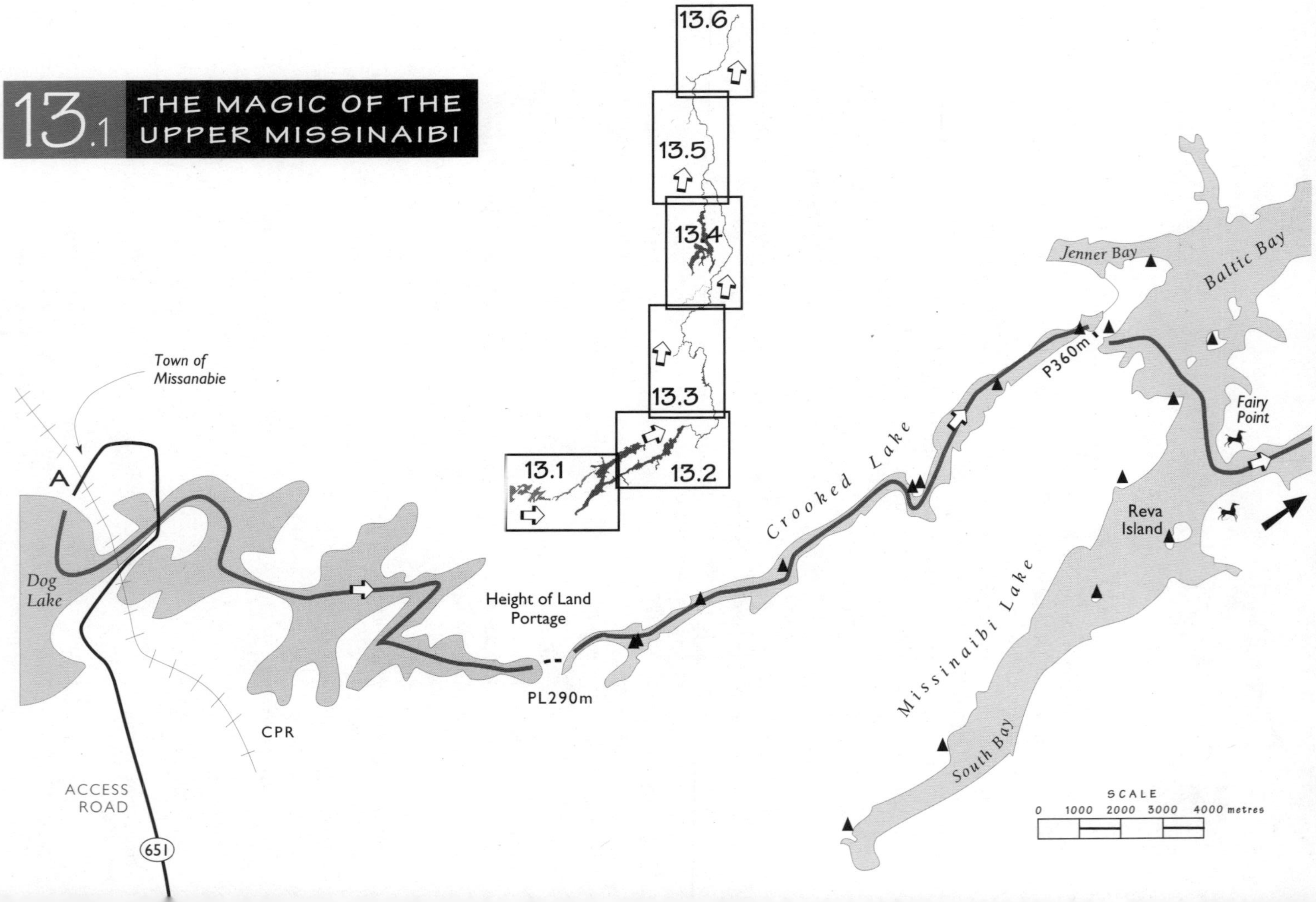

Town of Missanabie

Dog Lake

A

CPR

ACCESS ROAD

651

Height of Land Portage

PL290m

Crooked Lake

P360m

Jenner Bay

Baltic Bay

Fairy Point

Reva Island

Missinaibi Lake

South Bay

13.1

13.2

13.3

13.4

13.5

13.6

SCALE

0 1000 2000 3000 4000 metres

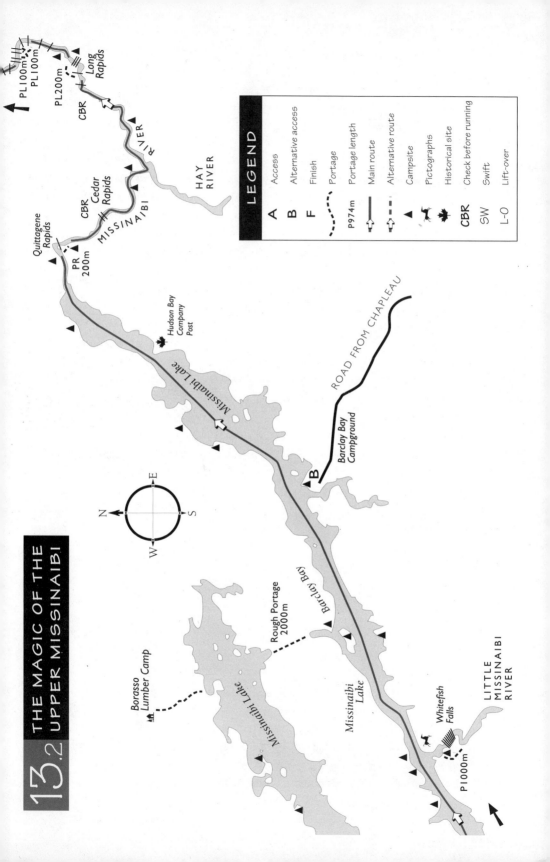

13.2 THE MAGIC OF THE UPPER MISSINAIBI

LEGEND

A		Access
B		Alternative access
F		Finish
		Portage
P974m		Portage length
		Main route
		Alternative route
		Campsite
		Pictographs
		Historical site
CBR		Check before running
SW		Swift
L-O		Lift-over

N / E / S / W

PL100m
PL100m
PL200m
CBR
Long Rapids

HAY RIVER

MISSINAIBI RIVER

Quittagene Rapids
CBR
Cedar Rapids
PR 200m

Hudson Bay Company Post

Missinaibi Lake

Barclay Bay Campground

B

ROAD FROM CHAPLEAU

Barclay Bay

Rough Portage 2000m

Borasso Lumber Camp

Missinaibi Lake

Missinaibi Lake

Whitefish Falls
P1000m

LITTLE MISSINAIBI RIVER

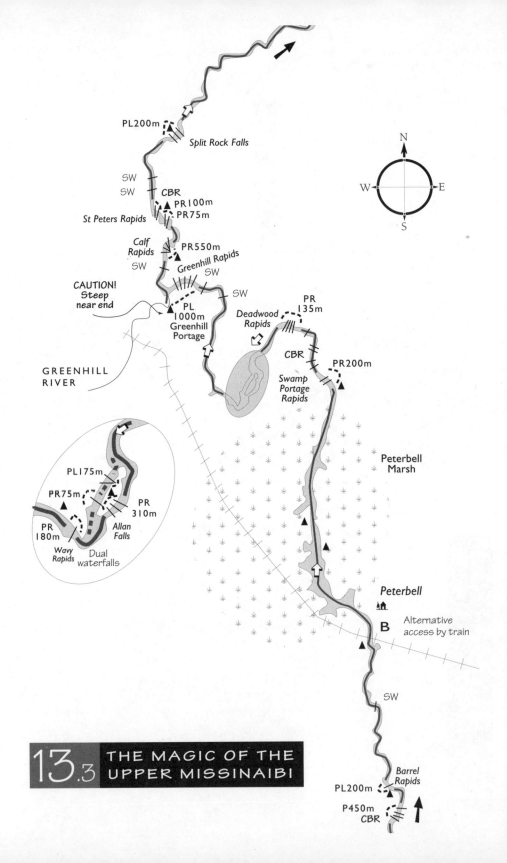

PL200m
Split Rock Falls

SW
SW   CBR
        PR100m
St Peters Rapids   PR75m

*Calf
Rapids*   PR550m
SW   *Greenhill Rapids*
                  SW

**CAUTION!
Steep
near end**   SW
                  PR
        PL   135m
        1000m   *Deadwood
        Greenhill   Rapids*
        Portage
                  CBR   PR200m

**GREENHILL
RIVER**   *Swamp
                  Portage
                  Rapids*

PL175m

PR75m   *Peterbell
PR   PR   Marsh*
310m

PR   *Allan
180m   Falls*

*Wavy   Dual
Rapids   waterfalls*

                  Peterbell

                  B   *Alternative
                  access by train*

                  SW

13.3 THE MAGIC OF THE
UPPER MISSINAIBI

                  *Barrel
                  Rapids*
        PL200m
        P450m
        CBR

N
W   E
S

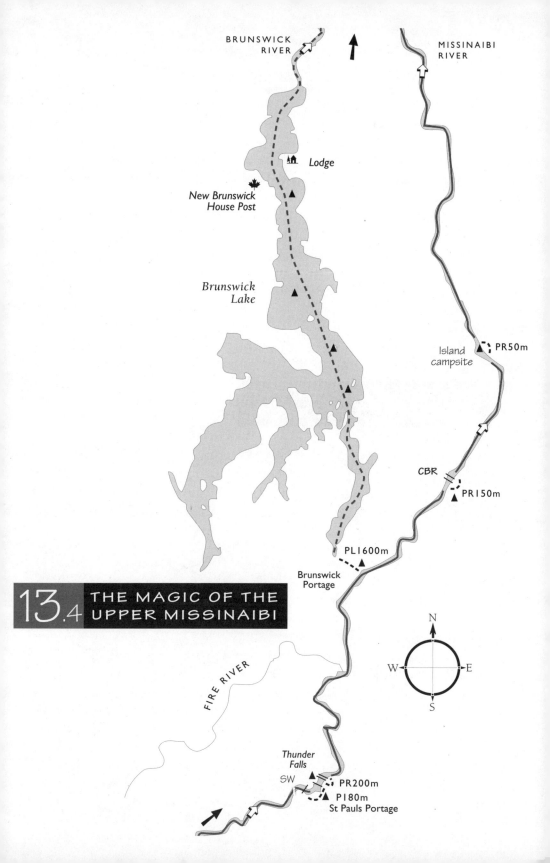

BRUNSWICK
RIVER

MISSINAIBI
RIVER

Lodge

New Brunswick
House Post

*Brunswick
Lake*

Island
campsite

PR50m

CBR

PR150m

PL1600m

Brunswick
Portage

FIRE RIVER

N

W   E

S

*Thunder
Falls*

SW

PR200m

P180m
St Pauls Portage

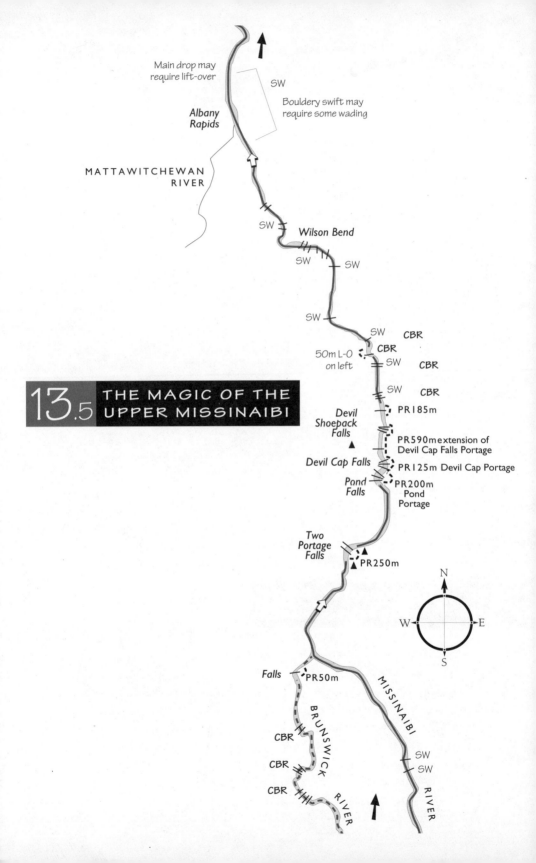

Main drop may
require lift-over

SW

Bouldery swift may
require some wading

*Albany
Rapids*

MATTAWITCHEWAN
RIVER

SW

Wilson Bend

SW   SW

SW

SW   CBR
CBR

50m L-O   CBR
on left   SW   CBR

SW   CBR

PR185m

13.5 THE MAGIC OF THE UPPER MISSINAIBI

*Devil
Shoepack
Falls*

PR590m extension of
Devil Cap Falls Portage

Devil Cap Falls   PR125m Devil Cap Portage

*Pond
Falls*   PR200m
Pond
Portage

*Two
Portage
Falls*   PR250m

N

W   E

S

Falls   PR50m

B R U N S W I C K
R I V E R

M I S S I N A I B I

CBR

CBR   SW
SW

CBR

R I V E R

13.6 THE MAGIC OF THE UPPER MISSINAIBI

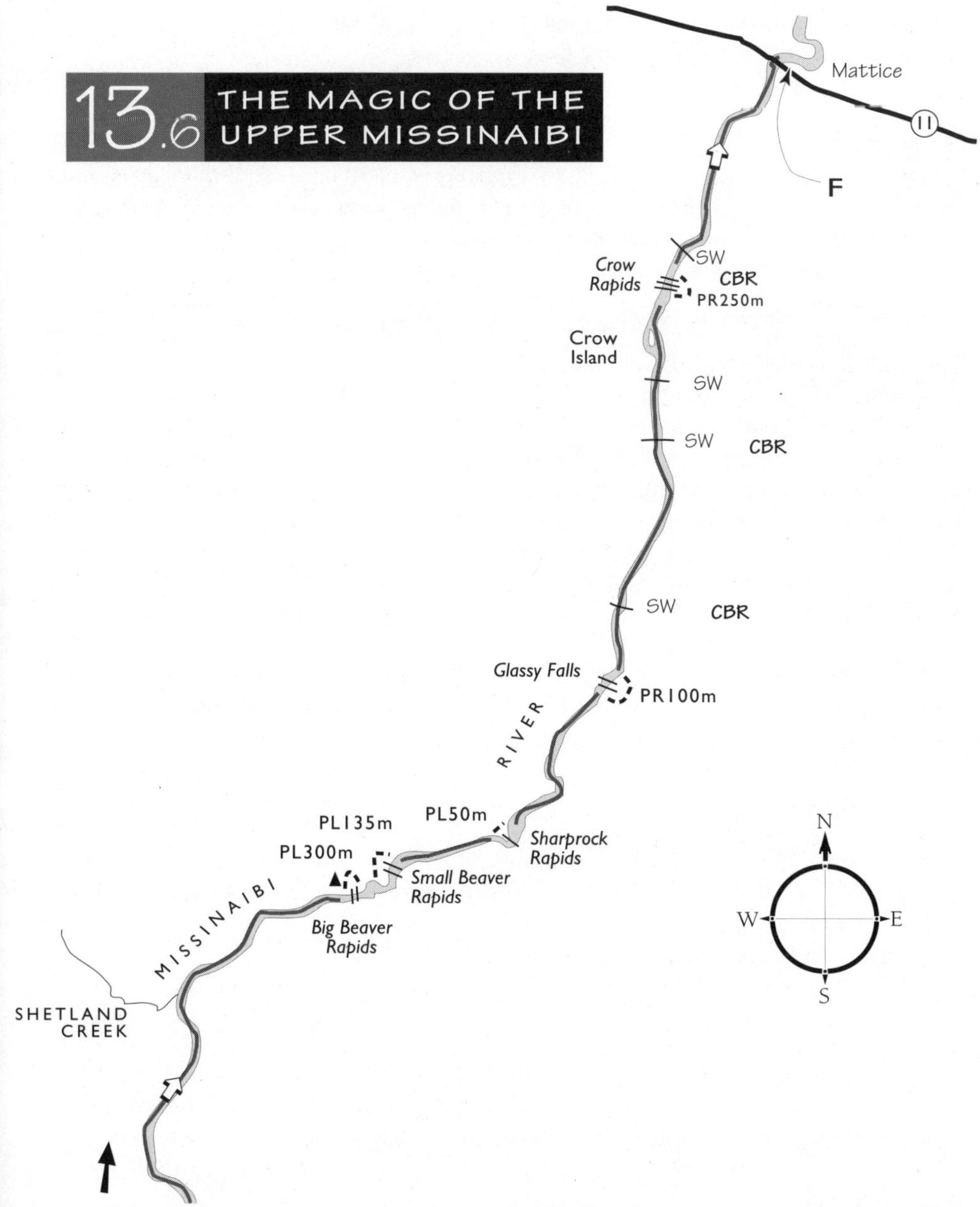

Mattice

(11)

F

Crow Rapids — SW — CBR — PR250m

Crow Island

SW

SW — CBR

SW — CBR

Glassy Falls — PR100m

RIVER

PL135m — PL50m

PL300m — Sharprock Rapids

Small Beaver Rapids

Big Beaver Rapids

MISSINAIBI

SHETLAND CREEK

N
W — E
S

I met Owen, the owner of Missinaibi Outfitters, at the put-in spot just before 9 a.m., after spending the night at Shoals Provincial Park along Highway 101. By 9:30 a.m. I had loaded up my canoe and handed over my truck keys to Owen, who, thinking that it would wise to warn me of the increase in bear problems along the river, marked the whereabouts of two reports of nuisance bruins on my map before wishing me good luck and getting into my pickup.

Owen's warning did nothing to ease the bear phobia I had been plagued with ever since I heard a report on the radio of a bear attack in the same area only two days before. The thirty-second news story told of a young geologist who, while crouching over to collect a soil sample, had been decapitated by a single blow of the bruin's paw. Apparently the predacious bear stalked the man, mistaking him for a moose calf — a dietary option for the bears when blueberry bushes become sterile from a late frost.

After waving a final goodbye to Owen I slipped into the canoe and headed east along Dog Lake, keeping an eye out for irritable bruins wandering the woods suffering from hunger cramps.

At the far eastern end of Dog Lake I portaged over a 290-metre path to Crooked Lake. The swampy trail is called Height of Land Portage and works its way over the division of land separating the Atlantic and Hudson Bay watersheds.

Approximately three quarters of the way along Crooked Lake, where the lake makes a sudden twist southeast, a number of good campsites can be found. One commonly used site is to the left of a demolished old bridge that once crossed the narrows. It was on this site that I spotted my first of the eight bears I encountered during my ten-day canoe trip. The bear was snacking on fish guts left by a group of anglers. I decided to leave the campsite to the bear, and paddled to the end of Crooked Lake to make camp.

Paddling from Dog Lake to the far end of Crooked Lake was a long stretch for the first day out, and, making dinner my first priority, the moment I beached my canoe I threw my food pack up onto the outcrop of rock. When the pack hit the hard surface I heard a horrific crack. It was my flask of Baileys Irish Cream that had broken, spilling out its gooey contents all over my gear. I spent the next hour trying to wash off my only supply of liquor from the rest of my supplies, wondering how well bears were attracted to sweet smell of Irish cream.

Early the next morning I took a short paddle from my campsite over to the portage heading from Crooked Lake into Missinaibi Lake. At the end of the 360-metre well-worn trail, I signed the Ministry of Natural Resources registration book and headed out into the headwaters of the 99,152-hectare provincial park.

Missinaibi Lake, its three main bays shaped like an elongated Y, stretches over 40 kilometres in length. It takes at least two days to reach the mouth of the Missinaibi River, to the northeast. A canoeist can spend an entire week exploring the lake. Visit Reva Island off South Bay to view the 350-year-old stands of white and red pine; fish for walleye at the base of Whitefish Falls; paddle upriver on the Little Missinaibi to explore the kettle formations decorated with unusual pictographs; or venture into the more isolated Baltic Bay to hike inland to the old Borasso lumber camp.

The buildings of the Borasso ghost camp were first floated down the bay in the early 1950s, on barges made from gigantic white pine, and then dragged in to the site by horse teams. A 3-kilometre trail works its way through thick stands of jack pine and spruce to the abandoned trail. Apart from the stables that have collapsed, it's the most intact lumber camp I've come across during my travels in the north. Still standing are the barracks, dining hall, kitchen and store (which housed a dusty receipt for gas and oil dated September and August

1957, three years before the camp was closed down). A well-positioned outhouse, scarred by numerous vertical bear claw marks, also stands erect in the centre of the camp. I was lucky enough to meet Fred, a retired wildlife officer who had worked in the area since 1947, while he and I were camped out on Missinaibi Lake. His site was directly across from mine, and after helping me chase "bear number two" from my camp, Fred had invited me over for a cup of coffee and a game of cribbage. Between games Fred talked about his life as a ranger in the area. Since the Chapleau Game Preserve (one of the largest preserves in the world) was established in 1925 to help keep a healthy stock of fur-bearing animals in the north, Fred had the job of checking local lumber camps for illegal guns. Every now and then the odd rifle was sneaked in by one of the men trying to make an extra dollar on the side.

Fred recalled one particular summer in the 1950s. He made a visit to one of the caretakers of a camp to the north of the lake, only to find the man had been driven insane by a marauding bear trying to break into the kitchen supplies. The caretaker had barricaded the windows with bedsprings and was sitting in the middle of the camp kitchen with a butcher knife gripped in his hand. A bear's claw was lying on the floor by one of the windows. "I'll never forget that night," Fred reminisced. "I sat by the window, armed with my rifle, and shot close to a dozen bears. The berries didn't ripen — just like they didn't this year — and every time I shot a bruin, another one would walk into my sights to feed off the previous carcass."

Needless to say, Fred's tales only heightened my bear phobia. It was good to know, however, that some years later Fred went from shooting bears to live-trapping them. In fact, he is the inventor of the bear trap usually employed in provincial parks across Ontario today.

If your time is limited you may not have the opportunity to visit the lumber camps, the Little Missinaibi River or Reva Island. But Fairy Point should not be missed. This sheer granite cliff is adorned with over a hundred Native pictographs. The best of three rock-painting sites on Missinaibi Lake, Fairy Point is the most extensive collection of pictographs in Northeastern Ontario, and one of the few in North America that has white-coloured symbols along with the customary red paintings of red ochre.

The rock paintings represent a number of symbols, including caribou, herons, soul boats used by shamans in search of lost souls, and even the legendary Mishipizhiw — the Great Lynx, who has the magic to conjure up storms and high winds.

Provoking Mishipizhiw is not something one should do while paddling the expanse of Missinaibi Lake, especially along the exposed Fairy Point. In minutes winds can sculpture metre-high waves and send them crashing against the rugged cliff.

Many canoeists have overturned, and even lost their lives, at the base of the steep rock wall at Fairy Point. Even larger fishing boats and their occupants have ended up at the bottom. The water is estimated to be 300 metres deep at Fairy Point. In the late 1980s, however, a one-person submarine searching for the body of a drowned fisherman at the base of the rock cliff discovered a series of seemingly bottomless caves and crevices.

I was lucky enough to paddle Missinaibi Lake on a calm, cloudless day. However, as I made my way across I met up with a Ministry of Natural Resources tugboat towing the wreck of a fishing boat that had crashed against the rocks during a freak snowstorm just a few days earlier. The fishermen had been marooned on an island for two days until help arrived.

The men had returned to the island to salvage the boat, equipped with a rented generator to pump out the water while the Ministry tug dragged the craft back to Barclay Bay Campground.

Enjoying soup and sandwiches (Allan Falls, Missinaibi River).

The comedy of the whole ordeal was that the tug ran out of gas just before the landing, and while the captain of the tug hurried to refill the gas tank, the owner of the sinking vessel jumped on board to attempt to bail out the excess water. Only the tip of the bow was break-ing the water's surface when the tug finally started up and yanked the boat free. The force of the pull, however, sent the fisherman flying into the drink along with his gear.

The captain of the tug, unable to stop and retrieve the man who fell overboard, motioned for me to lend him a hand. I'll never forget him. His fancy fishing boat was totally ruined, every piece of fishing gear and camping equipment and the rented generator gone to the bot-tom, and his only immediate concern was that his "smokes" didn't get wet.

Just before Barclay Bay, both shorelines are marked by an ugly fire-scar left by the great Missinaibi fire of 1987. The initial strike was a single lightning bolt. A strip of wilderness 21 kilometres long and 4 kilometres wide (a total of 7,500 hectares) was burned. The interior sites along the burn area were covered in thick brush, making them a haven for marauding bears. So I made the hasty decision to put up for the night among fellow campers at the main campground at Barclay Bay. Of course the moment dinner hour came and food smells per-meated the campground I quickly realized I would have been safer camped out in the wilds: a total of two bears (numbers three and four) ran through my campsite that evening, one with a loaf of bread in its mouth and the other with an entire roast chicken.

Around midnight I awoke to a strange snorting sound coming from just outside my tent. In my groggy state I mistook the intruder for one of the bears returning for dessert, and gave the nylon wall a slap with the palm of my hand to ward off the enemy. To my surprise, the animal outside slapped back, leaving a handful of tiny barbed quills behind, stuck into the side of the tent. I fumbled for my flashlight and poked my head outside the door in time to witness a very startled porcupine waddling back into the woods.

The next morning I was on the water bright and early, well before my neighbours attracted the local bear population with breakfast smells, and reached the sandy narrows at the far northeastern tip of Missinaibi Lake in time for brunch. I beached my canoe and set up my cookstove to fry up some bannock on the site of the historic Hudson Bay post. The buildings that once stood on the cleared grassy area signify the move inland of both the Hudson Bay Company, from its base camp at the mouth of the Moose River, and its rival, the North West Company, based on Lake Superior. Competition between the two trading companies and the need to forge better contacts with the Native people gave rise to this 140-year-old link between Hudson Bay and the Great Lakes by way of the Moose, Missinaibi, and Michipicoten Rivers, and it quickly became the most important transportation route in Northeastern Ontario.

The first attempt to establish a post on Missinaibi Lake was in 1777. The Hudson Bay Company dispatched John Thomas from Moose Factory, instructing him to travel inland in search of an ideal location to build an outpost. Missinaibi Lake was chosen for its good fishing and hunting possibilities, but during a three-year period Thomas and his men endured near starvation (they were reduced to eating beaver skins and dog meat) and severe cold winters, and were threatened with their lives by rivals from the North West Company as well as unfriendly Native people. Finally in 1780, during Thomas's absence, the Natives apparently were persuaded by the North West Company to force the two remaining men, John Leask and John Smith, to abandon the outpost and burn the buildings to the ground.

More effort was then devoted to the New Brunswick House on Brunswick Lake, but the post at Missinaibi was rebuilt in 1873 and remained in operation until 1917. The only vestiges of the post are the outlines of log buildings, now taken over by the open meadow, and a graveyard back in the bush where one grave marks the death of a five-year-old boy in 1897.

My break was shortlived after bear sighting number five. This time the bear was munching on a patch of clover less than a hundred metres from my beached canoe (I have a photo to prove it). I quickly leaped into my canoe, paddled through the last stretch of the grassy shallows, and began heading downriver on the Missinaibi.

Shortly after where the waterway begins, the river makes a dramatic turn to the right. Here the first portage of the river section allows you to avoid running Quittagene Rapids. The 200-metre trail is marked along the right bank, just after a washed-out dam and bridge left behind from the logging era.

From Quittagene Rapids to Barrel Rapids, where I spent my first night camped on the river, the character of the Missinaibi is mixed. The slow-moving current, gurgling past cedar-lined banks and the marshy mouth of the Hay River, is interrupted by six sets of rapids and a number of swifts — all of which are runnable except possibly the fifth set, where the river rounds a bend. Two 100-metre portages, following in succession, can be found along the left bank.

By the time I reached Barrel Rapids, there was just enough light in the day to scramble up the beginning of the muddy 200-metre portage along the left bank, pitch my tent and crawl inside my cosy sleeping bag.

Later that night, I discovered the dangers of setting up camp in the middle of a portage trail. Around 2 a.m. I went to exit my tent to answer the call of nature and spotted a bull moose standing just outside the front flap, studying the strange dome-shaped object blocking his path. It was a long couple of minutes before he decided to backtrack and search out an alternative route down to the river.

Next day after a breakfast of hot cereal and "true grit" coffee, I completed the Barrel Rapids portage during a heavy downpour of hailstones. Imagine! The first week in July and I found myself deafened by large ice-balls bouncing off the canoe balanced over my shoulders.

Fortunately the storm didn't last, and I spent the afternoon floating down toward the expanse of Peterbell Marsh, dangling my socks over the gunwale to dry.

Just before the extensive marshland, where the Canadian National Railway bridge crosses the river, I went in search of any signs of the once-thriving community of Peterbell. The ghost town, at one time home to over two hundred people, was established in an attempt to promote agriculture in the Clay Belt area. Land was cleared for only a few kilometres on both sides of the railway track, however, and the hamlet's interest turned to the area's logging boom in the 1920s. The boom finally went to bust, forcing the sawmill to close down in 1962.

It was also here at the Peterbell station that a group of elk were introduced to the area. In 1933, on its way out west, a train transporting elk dropped their cargo off well before their destination of Mainwright, Alberta, when it was noted that a sickness was spreading throughout the entire herd. The small group somehow managed not to perish and their offspring are sometimes spotted in the open areas of Hay River or Missinaibi House.

Make sure to slow your pace as you paddle through Peterbell Marsh. This complex wetland, home to a host of wildlife, and run through with numerous channels, is breaking away from the main waterway as a result of the current and the efforts of beaver. Floating down that smooth water, I startled black ducks and sandpipers as my canoe rounded the slower bends, watched a bald eagle soar majestically overhead, and spied on a cow moose and her calf feeding in an isolated bog.

To me, the most awe-inspiring sight of the Peterbell Marsh is the clear transition from open wetland to dry, ridgetop habitat. In many places the flat horizon of swamp is broken by bluffs clad in pine and birch, providing excellent sites to pitch a tent.

Eventually, the current quickens its pace as it heads for Swamp Rapids. A 200-metre portage is located along the right bank, just past an old trapper's cabin. The next five sets of rapids can be run or lined, but be cautious at the fifth, called Deadwood Rapids. You should take the 135-metre portage to the right if you think the run is questionable.

Downriver from Deadwood Rapids the river splits into two channels, washing around Allan Island. The right channel is broken up by a logjam and a pile of jagged rocks. A 175-metre portage works its way around the blockade of logs to the left, and a 75-metre portage may be necessary on the right to avoid the rock garden if water levels are low.

The left channel has only a single, 310-metre portage, located to the right of a stunted cascade (Allan Falls). A perfect campsite can also be found at the take-out, making it the better choice of the two channels if it is late in the day.

To a whitewater fanatic, the next section of the river would be the most challenging and exciting. Travelling solo, however, I opted to keep to the gruelling portages. The first is a 180-metre path to the right of Wavy Rapids. The name is appropriate, as there are high-standing waves gushing down the gut of the rapid. If you chance the run, be prepared to take some water over the bow.

Greenhill Rapids is next. I bypassed this section of whitewater by using the 1,000-metre portage to the left. The carry through the bush is a lengthy and difficult one, but the rapid itself is encased by steep banks on either side, making it impossible to turn tail once you begin the run.

The next portage is marked to the right of Calf Rapids. The previous year, hurricane winds had left the entire 550-metre trail cluttered with fallen trees. I was physically exhausted by the time I reached the next set — St. Peters Rapids — and opted to avoid using the 75-metre and 100-metre portages both on the right. I cautiously steered between half-submerged boulders, grinding the bottom of the canoe only once while trying to dodge the rocky shallows on one of the two swifts that follow shortly after the main drop.

After St. Peter's Rapids comes Split Rock Falls. A 200-metre portage with a scenic campsite near the put-in point is marked to the left of this stunted cascade. After a day of slogging along portages, I was eager to carry my gear over to the campsite and finish the day early. As I crested a hill midway along the portage, however, I startled a bear. The beast took off through the bush, but the sighting (number six if you're still counting) gave me second thoughts about camping at Split Rock, and I ended up paddling another 10 kilometres downriver to set up camp at Thunder Falls.

Just before the portage, marked on the right of Thunder Falls, there are two easy swifts that must be navigated through. Here, it's important to stay to the right bank until you reach the small bay where the 180-metre path, called St. Paul's Portage, begins. A small campsite is marked directly above the muddy embankment at the take-out. However, it's best to complete the portage and paddle to a nicer sandy tent site across the river.

Almost immediately following Thunder Falls, another portage (200 metres) makes its way along the right of a second, less dramatic falls.

After the last drop in the river, the mood of the waterway changes, and it is seemingly still for a great distance. Only by peering down at the bent grasses rooted in the riverbed could one tell that the water was still alive.

Further downriver, past where the Fire River joins up with the Missinaibi, a single strip of red ribbon marks the 1,600-metre portage to Brunswick Lake. From this point you must make the decision to either stay with the river or carry over to visit Brunswick Lake.

If you choose to portage into Brunswick Lake, be prepared to get your feet wet. The last 100 metres or so is cursed with knee-deep boot-sucking swamp ooze. But the lake itself, with its pine island campsites, can be the highlight of the trip.

At the far northwestern tip of the lake lies the now-empty site of the former Hudson Bay post. Today only a meadow marks the spot where the Hudson Bay Company and the North West Company battled for superiority in the fur trade. The New Brunswick House was occupied by the Hudson Bay Company between 1788 and 1879, and is now regarded as one of the most important archaeological sites in Northern Ontario.

To exit Brunswick Lake, paddle north, following the Brunswick River. All the rapids along the river are runnable, thanks to past voyageurs who dredged out a clear channel for their large trade canoes, all except for a one-metre-high falls close to where the Brunswick River joins up with the Missinaibi. A 50-metre portage can be found to the right of the cascade.

I chose to avoid Brunswick Lake and stay with the river — not because of the muddy portage, but rather due to bear number seven, sighted at the take-out.

This stretch of the river is clogged with low-lying cedar rooted along the banks, and the odd swift en route to break up the relatively soft-flowing current. An island set in the middle of the waterway, approximately 10 kilometres downstream from the Brunswick portage, makes an excellent place to camp. To reach the site, take the 50-metre portage along the right bank and paddle over to the island from the put-in.

From the island campsite to the place where an unsightly iron bridge appears, the river seems somewhat monotonous. Only two fast swifts, halfway along, propel your canoe further downstream.

Then, beyond the mouth of the Brunswick River, a 250-metre portage to the right works its way around Two Portage Falls. There is an adequate campsite along the portage, but I prefer the site at Pond Falls. Keep a watchful eye on the current here. The 200-metre portage along the right bank begins dangerously close to the brink of the falls.

The long stretch of whitewater below Pond Falls can be a graveyard for canoes. Aptly named, the first drop, Devil Cap Falls, can be portaged (125 metres) to the right. A 590-metre portage, also along the right bank, follows. The path allows you to avoid running the rock-strewn Devil Shoepack Rapids. Two short cascades remain; the first with a 185-metre portage to the right and the second, a 50-metre lift-over to the left.

Downstream the river's quickened pace remains constant, making its way around Wilson Bend, and then for 3 kilometres, through a boulder garden called Albany Rapids. Here, you must slowly manoeuvre your way like an Olympic skier on a slalom run. Only the last swift needs special attention, and you may wish to lift over here. (More than one canoeist has drowned at the deadly sluice-hole at the base of the drop.)

The geology of the area begins to change after Albany Rapids. Big Beaver Rapids, Small Beaver Rapids, Sharprock Rapids and Glassy Falls all flow over fragmented bedrock. The sharp-edged souvenirs from the early Precambrian era make this one of the most scenic stretches en route, but can also make your canoe's hull seem fragile as an eggshell. Portages for the first three sets of rapids are along the left bank (300 metres, 135 metres, and a steep 50 metres). Glassy Falls portage (100 metres) is to the right and ends at a beautiful sandy beach.

A couple of shallow swifts and the navigable Crow Rapids (where yet another bear crossed my path as it swam downstream, only 30 metres from my bow) bring the only interruptions in the slackened river current before you reach the riverside municipal park at Mattice. It is here that you will begin to notice small signs of the upcoming town: bottles and cans embedded in the river's sandy bottom; tire ruts from ATV vehicles worn into the muddy shoreline; the sounds of buzzing chain saws, barking dogs, and traffic zooming along Highway 11.

The government dock at Mattice marked the end of my incredible adventure down the Missinaibi, and as I enjoyed a fresh cup of coffee at the local restaurant, waiting for Owen from Missinaibi Outfitters to arrive with my truck, I glanced through the logbook the cafe has on hand for canoeists to sign after their trip down the river. I went through three cups of coffee and two slices of pie before I figured out what to jot down beside my signature. I wrote: "The spirits are still alive and well on the Missinaibi!"

TIME:
10 to 12 days

DIFFICULTY:
Canoeists must be experienced trippers, with a moderate to high level of experience running whitewater. The majority of rapids can be portaged. However, maintenance of the route by the Ministry of Natural Resources is inadequate at times, and some portages may not be clearly marked. Crossing Missinaibi Lake can also be extremely dangerous if the wind picks up.

PORTAGES:
29

LONGEST PORTAGE:
1,600 metres (Brunswick Lake), and 1,000 metres (Greenhill Rapids)

FEE:
For Canadian citizens there is presently no fee required for paddling through Missinaibi Provincial Park. A campsite permit must be purchased at the gatehouse if you decide to stay over at the Barclay Bay Campground on Missinaibi Lake. As well, a moderate fee is charged for the shuttle service.

ALTERNATIVE ACCESS:
Canoeists may access the route at either the Barclay Bay Campground on Missinaibi Lake or at the Peterbell train bridge. To reach Barclay Bay Campground, however, you must drive north of Chapleau on a 88-kilometre gravel road, and it is a pain to organize a shuttle from the campground. Accessing the river at Peterbell by train can also be a bother. The scheduled times of the train are sketchy, and in the future the train may not even stop at Peterbell.

ALTERNATIVE ROUTE:
If you drive north of Chapleau to the Barclay Bay Campground on Missinaibi Lake, you can spend an entire week exploring the surrounding area.

OUTFITTERS:
Missinaibi Outfitters
Box 2311
Hearst, Ontario
P0L 1N0
(705) 364-7312
(summer)

Missinaibi Headwaters Outfitters
Winter address:
R.R. 1 Poplar Sideroad
Collingwood, Ontario
L9Y 3Y9
(705) 444-7780

July & August address:
General Delivery
Chapleau, Ontario
P0M 1K0
(705) 864-2065

FOR MORE INFORMATION:
Ministry of Natural Resources
190 Cherry Street
Chapleau, Ontario
P0M 1K0
(705) 864-1710

MAPS:
The Ministry of Natural Resources has produced a canoe route pamphlet, *Missinaibi River Canoe Route*. Hap Wilson's guide book, *Missinaibi: Journey to the Northern Sky*, published by the Canadian Recreational Canoeing Association, is also an excellent reference.

TOPOGRAPHIC MAPS:
42 C/8, 42 B/5, 42 B/6, 42 B/11, 42 B/14, 42 G/3, 42 G/6, 42 G/11W

Alana cooks up her specialty — pita pizza (Batchewaung Bay, Quetico).

14 The Wilds of Quetico

My wife and I felt out of place as we waited in line inside the gatehouse at Quetico Provincial Park's Nym Lake access point. The groups ahead of us, who were obviously park regulars, rattled off their one-week itineraries as if they were school outings. Alana and I, however, had never visited Quetico before, and when it was our turn to pay the permit fee we stood there dumbfounded when the gate attendant asked, "So, where ya headed?"

The park staff was polite, considering that the line of canoeists behind us had lengthened to outside the gatehouse and down the front steps while we took time to look over the provincial park map taped to the wall. We found ourselves overwhelmed by the size of it all, by the prospect of trying to plot out a route with so many tangled lakes and streams to explore.

But as I traced out countless imaginary routes, I couldn't help but notice a number of black pins stuck in clusters all over the map. Curiosity got the better of me and I found myself taking valuable time to ask the employee behind the desk what the black pinheads represented. The gate attendant, still relatively calm as the line of canoeists now extended out to the parking lot, replied, "Those are this month's nuisance bear reports." Of course, I had to ask, "How do you define a nuisance bear?" "Well," she stated, with all seriousness, "the bruin has to either tear open a tent or walk away with a food pack before it's labelled a nuisance."

So, there you have it. In less than thirty seconds Alana and I laid out our five-day canoe route by simply connecting a series of lakes free of black pinheads, creating an excellent introductory trip into the wilds of Quetico Provincial Park — and we came out of it with our tent and food pack still intact.

The Nym Lake access point, located on the north side of the park (east of Atikokan), can be reached by turning south off Highway 11 onto Nym Lake Road. Then turn left onto a dirt road, before a Y-intersection. The road ends at a designated parking lot, just beyond the park gatehouse.

Admittance to Quetico's interior is managed by a quota system (the point of entry does not restrict where you go or how long you go for), and the Nym Lake access is one of the most popular entry points to the park, so make sure to phone or write to make a reservation well in advance (Canadian residents call 807-597-2735 and U.S. residents call 807-597-2735).

It is also important to note that the interior program for Quetico Provincial Park is like no other in the province. To enhance the canoeist's wilderness experience, campsites and portages are not marked in the interior. With that in mind, you can camp anywhere within the boundaries of the park so long as you practise low-impact camping. We found, however, that most lakes had campsites that were obvious because of regular use from previous years, and that the majority of portages were easily located by looking for patches of trampled earth and streaks of canoe paint scratched on top of rocks.

This "wilderness concept" can be frustrating at times. If you want to be guaranteed a prime campsite it is crucial that you stop to make camp by late afternoon. And to make locating the take-out for the portage less of an ordeal, you may find it rewarding to practise up on your map and compass skills prior to the trip.

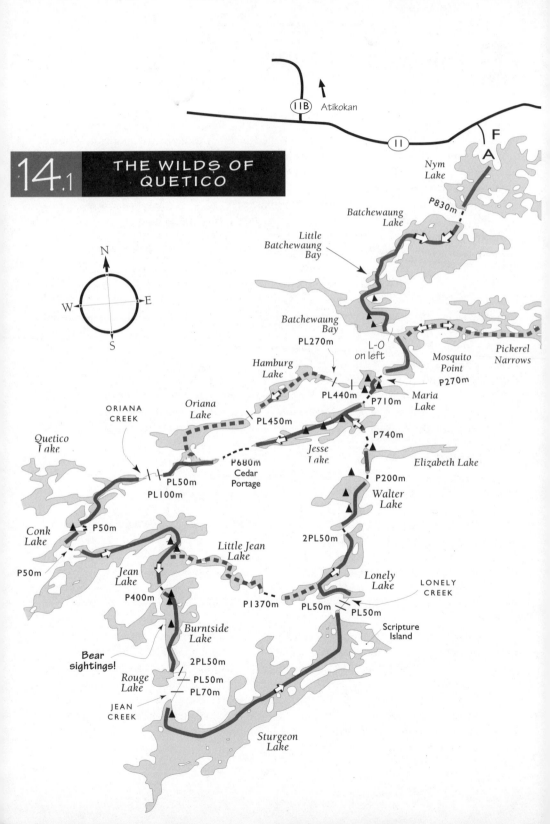

11B Atikokan

11

F

A

Nym Lake

P830m

Batchewaung Lake

Little Batchewaung Bay

Batchewaung Bay

PL270m

L-O on left

Mosquito Point

Pickerel Narrows

P270m

Hamburg Lake

PL440m

Maria Lake

P710m

Oriana Lake

PL450m

ORIANA CREEK

P740m

Jesse Lake

Elizabeth Lake

Quetico Lake

P680m Cedar Portage

PL50m
PL100m

P200m

Walter Lake

Conk Lake

P50m

Little Jean Lake

2PL50m

P50m

Jean Lake

Lonely Lake

P400m

P1370m

PL50m

LONELY CREEK

Burntside Lake

PL50m

Scripture Island

Bear sightings!

2PL50m

Rouge Lake

PL50m
PL70m

JEAN CREEK

Sturgeon Lake

N
W E
S

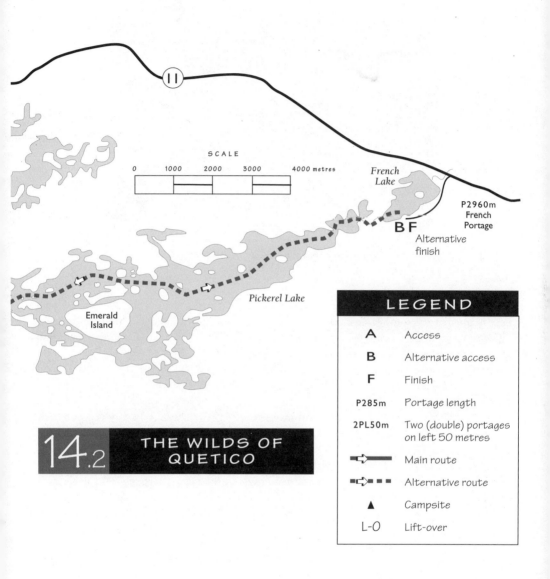

SCALE

0   1000   2000   3000   4000 metres

French
Lake

P2960m
French
Portage

B F

Alternative
finish

Pickerel Lake

Emerald
Island

14.2 THE WILDS OF QUETICO

LEGEND

A	Access
B	Alternative access
F	Finish
P285m	Portage length
2PL50m	Two (double) portages on left 50 metres
⇨	Main route
⇨	Alternative route
▲	Campsite
L-O	Lift-over

Common mergansers fish the weedy shoreline of Jesse Lake.

To begin the route you must first portage down to the dock on Nym Lake, following a path marked at the southeastern corner of the parking lot. From the dock, head south, making your way through a cluster of islands and to the 830-metre portage that crosses over into the park's northern boundary and leads to Batchewaung Lake.

This portage is typical of all portages in Quetico — mildly rolling terrain interrupted on occasion by a sharp incline or a patch of slimy, waist-deep mud with the odd log thrown across to keep you from sinking.

From Batchewaung Lake, paddle southwest to Little Batchewaung Bay by way of a shallow narrows. Turn left near the end of the inlet, where a channel opens up into the expanse of Batchewaung Bay.

It was at Batchewaung Bay's southeastern end, where we stopped for soup and tea on a small scenic island, that I spotted our first bald eagle of the trip. I happened to glance up at the clouding sky, wondering if the rain would hold off, and noticed the bird of prey soaring high above in a thermal of warm air, its white head and tail feathers bright against the grey overcast sky.

The route continues on from Batchewaung Bay to Pickerel Narrows by way of a rockbound channel. There is a double set of small rapids, but only if the water level has dropped will you have to step out of your canoe and either wade downstream or carry your gear along the left bank a short distance.

Once you've entered Pickerel Narrows, head south past Mosquito Point and then west to the end of the isolated bay, where a 270-metre portage, equipped with an extremely muddy take-out, leads directly into Maria Lake.

Alana and I spent our first night in Quetico camped on a rock outcrop just south of the portage. We were lucky when the rain held off and the clouds scudded across the sky to unveil incredible clusters of stars. By midnight the moon was shining through the canopy of jack pine circling our tent and a lone wolf howled in the distance.

The next morning we awoke early and decided to follow the route west by portaging the 710 metres into Jesse Lake instead of hop-skipping over beaver dams along the creek flowing out of Hamburg Lake (an option some canoeists prefer).

The path (beginning on the right side of the lake, where a stream trickles into the southern inlet) was unbelievably muddy, despite the lack of rain. At first I attempted to jump clear of the worst spots along the trail. But after a few tumbles with the weight of the canoe crashing down on my head, I decided to take the plunge and walk straight through the muck, conceding that being knee-deep in brown-coloured ooze was simply a Quetico tradition. Once you have made it through the mudbath, Jesse Lake offers some excellent opportunities for wildlife viewing, especially near the shallows at the east end. Just before the take-out for Cedar Portage, Alana and I were fortunate enough to see the antics of three river otters. We happened to spook the weasels, causing them to quickly jump off a rock ledge and into the lake. The first two leaped into the water with the grace of Olympic divers. The third, however, managed to trip on a small pebble at the edge of the rock face and flopped into the lake, belly first. We couldn't help but laugh at the poor fellow as his comrades stood high in the water, their heads up like periscopes, wondering what on earth had happened to their clumsy partner.

Cedar Portage measures 680 metres and leads into the south bay of Oriana Lake. Paddle directly west to Oriana Creek, where two short portages (50 metres and 100 metres) are found to the left.

The second of the two short portages ends where Oriana Creek tumbles into the eastern arm of Quetico Lake. The lake itself is huge, with the main body of water situated to the west. To stay en route, however, you must paddle south into a large bay (look for three small islands clustered together near the entrance).

A short but steep portage is located near the bay's southwest corner. The take-out is to the right of a 10-metre cascade gushing out of Conk Lake. Look for the rusted debris of Quetico's logging era scattered along the shoreline at both the take-out and put-in.

After a quick paddle across Conk Lake another short portage will take you into Jean Lake. If you're lucky, the wind will be coming from the west, sailing you down to a sandy peninsula popular for setting up camp, just ahead of the entrance to the lake's large southern bay.

Eager to take advantage of the good weather and get more distance behind us, Alana and I decided to continue on, across the 400-metre portage from Jean Lake to Burntside Lake (look for the old ranger's cabin at the put-in). After a long ten-hour day it was disappointing, to say the least, when we discovered the first three island campsites already occupied, the first two by canoeists and the third by a marauding bear.

It was close to 8 p.m. by the time we found a suitable spot on a tiny island to the south end of Burntside. By the dim light of our candle lantern, Alana erected the tent while I marked the exact whereabouts of our "nuisance" bear so the gate attendant back at Nym Lake could add another pin to the map on the wall.

Forewarned about the possible rough water out on Sturgeon Lake, Alana and I were up bright and early the next day to take advantage of the calm. We paddled through the narrows at Burntside's southern end, entered Rouge Lake, and then navigated Jean Creek by carrying over four short portages (all along the left bank), lifted over the odd beaver dam, and paddled around a huge bull moose standing in midstream.

In this case, however, the early bird didn't get the worm. As we paddled into the expanse of Sturgeon Lake, rain pelted down hard on the water and high winds began to whip up whitecaps on every second or third wave. Feeling somewhat distraught, we tried to make the best of the situation by beaching our canoe at the back of a bay, and under a saggy tarp we cooked up a filling brunch of camp coffee and flapjacks. While waiting for each pancake top to bubble, I would race back to the rocky shoreline, watching for the slightest change in the weather. Finally, after we had fried up two bowls of batter and consumed a considerable stack of pancakes, the pitch of the wind started to die down and we decided to pack up our cookset and tempt our fate out on the water.

The wind was blowing from the south, forcing us to battle directly into the gust as we exited the back bay. Then, by keeping close to the north shore, we crept slowly toward Sturgeon Lake's more protected eastern end. Along the way, when we were forced to head out directly across the gaping mouths of three large bays, I adjusted the direction of our bow in response to each oncoming wave. Most of the time the canoe would respond well, plunging through the rough water. There were some dicey moments, however, when I would misjudge the angle and size of the roiled water and a white spray would find its way over the gunwale.

Once we navigated through the narrows at the east end of Sturgeon Lake, before Scripture Island, we pointed the bow of the canoe to the northeast, toward the portage into Lonely Creek. With the wind now almost directly behind us, the canoe literally surfed on top of the ruffled water. Ten minutes later we found ourselves drifting in a tranquil lagoon setting, where Lonely Creek trickles into the weedy basin to the right of the portage. Alana leapt to shore the moment the bow grated up on the pebble beach, leaving me to crawl over the packs while she raced over to the nearest tree, gave it a hug, and like a shipwrecked sailor, yelled out, "Land! Land!"

The high winds had ruined our original plan to spend the entire day exploring historic Sturgeon Lake. Throughout the 1800s the lake was a busy highway. Ojibwa raiding parties paddled across the lake on their way to engage in bitter warfare with the Sioux; French-Canadian voyageurs travelled west from the Grand Portage; the Red River Expedition, a military expedition made up of Canadian Militia and British Regulars, headed toward the Red River Settlement to avenge the death of Thomas Scott, who was executed by the Métis leader, Louis Riel. Pioneers heading to Manitoba by way of the Dawson Trail, named after Simon J. Dawson, who originally charted the immigration route in 1857, traversed the lake by way of steam barges fuelled by a wood yard on the long island southwest of Scripture Island.

From the take-out on Sturgeon Lake the route travels north, up Lonely Creek. Two steep portages (both measuring approximately 50 metres) lead you into and then out of the shallow stream. Then, at the northeast end of Lonely Lake, the route follows over two more steep but short portages into Walter Lake.

It was late afternoon by the time Alana and I made it to Walter, and in the distance we could hear thunder rumbling ominously. So we quickly began to search the western shoreline for a safe haven for the night. We passed a somewhat inhospitable campsite, far back in a patch of dense spruce trees, but I urged that we press on to an island farther north. Halfway across, however, the weather turned grey and squally, and by the time we pulled the canoe ashore the storm was dangerously close.

First we secured the rain tarp, and then, while Alana set up the tent, I ran off into the backwoods to gather dry firewood, both of us feeling quite proud of the fact that we had raced against the elements and won — or so we thought! Three minutes later I came running back to camp to tell Alana that a bear was sharing the island with us.

So, with bolts of lightning cracking overhead and hard rain pelting down on the lake, the second "nuisance" bear of the trip forced us to pack our bags and head back out into the storm to camp at the previous site. We took advantage of being stormbound by spending time cooking up seconds of cinnamon rolls for dessert, and then dipped into the last of our Irish Cream liqueur as we played round after round of cribbage.

The storm had drifted off by morning, leaving us with clear skies but muddy portages, the first one located in the northeast corner of Walter Lake. The trail climbs steeply for approximately 200 metres before reaching Elizabeth Lake.

Paddling straight across to the small northern inlet on Elizabeth you will come to the next portage, a 740-metre mudbath, leading to familiar Jesse Lake.

Depending on the amount of time spent battling wind and waves during the past few days, you can either spend the rest of the day retracing your steps from the northeastern end of Jesse Lake and back to the access point on Nym Lake, or if you happen to be a day ahead of schedule, why not stop halfway and make camp on Batchewaung Bay. After a quick paddle the next morning, you'll have an early start for the long drive home.

TIME:
5 to 6 days

DIFFICULTY:
There are many large lakes en route and battling high winds may be a problem; canoeists must have at least a moderate level of tripping experience and be able to navigate by way of a map and compass.

PORTAGES:
24

LONGEST PORTAGE:
830 metres

FEE:
You must purchase an interior camping permit at the Ranger's Station before entering Quetico Provincial Park.

ALTERNATIVE ACCESS:
French Lake Campground

ALTERNATIVE ROUTES:
You can avoid paddling Sturgeon Lake and shorten your trip by one or two days by taking a shortcut from Jean Lake to Lonely Lake. Take the short portage from Little Jean Lake into Yeh Lake, and then the 1,370-metre portage from Yeh Lake into Lonely Lake. Another route is to begin at the French River Campground, off Highway 11, and connect up with the loop beginning at Maria Lake by way of French Lake, Pickerel Lake and then Pickerel Narrows.

OUTFITTERS:
Canoe Canada Outfitters
Box 1810
Atikokan, Ontario
P0T 1C0
(807) 597-6418

Quetico Discovery Tours
Box 593, 18 Birch Road
Atikokan, Ontario
P0T 1C0
(807) 597-2621

Quetico North Tourist Services
Box 100
Atikokan, Ontario
P0T 1C0
(807) 929-3561

FOR MORE INFORMATION:
Quetico Provincial Park
Ministry of Natural Resources
Atikokan, Ontario
P0T 1C0
(807) 597-2430 (information)
(807) 597-2735 (reservations for U.S. residents)
(807) 597-2737 (reservations for Canadian residents)

MAPS:
The Friends of Quetico and the Ministry of Natural Resources have produced an excellent waterproof map of Quetico's interior. *A Paddler's Guide to Quetico Provincial Park*, by Robert Beymer, is also an excellent guide for canoeing the park.

TOPOGRAPHIC MAPS:
52-B/11, 52-B/12, 52-B/13, 52-B/5

An unbelievable calm lasted for the entire five days John and I paddled the rugged shoreline of Lake Superior.

15 Paying Homage to Lake Superior

I'll never forget the first time John and I experienced the magical powers of Lake Superior. We were paddling out of the mouth of the White River with some colleagues, all of us feeling the ill effects of a can of toxic oysters I had packed, and as we leaned over to retch into the water, John and I observed flat-bottomed clouds drifting across from the west. Wind patches soon appeared on the once-smooth surface and swells quickly began to lift and deepen. Then swirling wind flicked ice-cold water off the crests of the waves and into our now flimsy-seeming canoe. Within minutes the lake shifted from a gentle undulation to a jostling of bottomless swells and tumbling breakers.

After witnessing such a drastic change of conditions, it is easy to feel some understanding of the Ojibwa belief that Superior is a major spiritual centre, an enchanted place regarded with deep veneration, where one must give homage in order to travel without peril.

So, on a return trip, this time joining John's daughter Kerry and friend Grace, visiting from New York, to paddle Lake Superior Provincial Park's coastline, we ceremoniously tossed an offering of tobacco into the lake before heading up the coast. We felt somewhat sceptical at first, even joking about how we resorted to using a cheap cigar we had purchased at a roadside cafe. But when we were done and headed out on Superior, it was as if the unrehearsed ceremony had rewarded us with a sort of calm assurance, a sense that we had done something right.

Originally we had planned to paddle the park's remote Sand River. Once we arrived, however, we quickly discovered the effects of a three-week dry spell. The river had been transformed from a rushing waterway into a dried-up boulder garden.

Disappointed, we sombrely chose to cancel the river trip and began making the necessary arrangements for travelling up the coast. By noon we had paid for an interior camping permit at the Agawa Bay gatehouse, shuttled a second vehicle down the 12-kilometre bush road to Gargantua Bay, and then parked along the west side of Highway 17 to unpack our gear at the Coldwater–June Creek access point.

The first day out we took advantage of an unusually calm Lake Superior and paddled close to the heaped boulders and steep, jagged cliffs of Bald Head Point, taking time out to collect multicoloured rocks, identifying various species of raptors hunting flocks of shorebirds, and snapping photos of ancient Arctic plants rooted in inhospitable knobs of granite. We had an extended lunch stop on the cobble terrace at the mouth of the Baldhead River, where the Group of Seven's Lawren Harris once depicted the rugged shore of Superior on canvas, and then paddled up to the twin falls for a refreshing swim.

It was only 3 p.m. when we pitched our tents at the designated campsite in Beatty Cove, a crescent of sheltered water screened from the expanse of the lake by a 70-metre-long raised beach. Enjoying the hot sun beaming down on the sandy shore and the slight breeze that was keeping the bugs at bay, we no longer felt disheartened about abandoning the river trip. Life out on Superior was far better than dragging a canoe down a dried-up riverbed.

The calm persisted the next day, with only a slight breeze barely ruffling the surface of the lake. We continued north, enjoying brunch on a small island, mop-topped with stunted

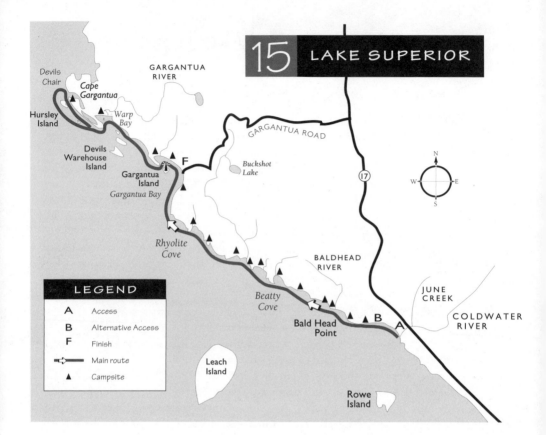

timber, and then spent two full hours investigating the reddish rock mass north of Rhyolite Cove. The bizarre geological structure marks the place where the 2.5-billion-year-old granite rocks and the 1-billion-year-old volcanic rocks meet. This gap of time represents one of the most extensive periods of erosion along the coast.

After our shoreline excursion the group decided to call it a day and we paddled around to the campsites in Gargantua Bay. At the entrance to the protective inlet, however, Kerry and Grace suddenly steered their canoe back toward shore. At first, John and I figured they had gone inland for a pee stop. But after waiting out in the swells for nearly half an hour we decided to check things out. One hundred metres away we could see Grace bent over and vomiting onto a slab of rock.

I was worried that it might be food poisoning, and said so. "Well, we all ate the same thing at that grease pit up the highway," John replied. "I guess we'll all know in the next twenty-four hours."

For Grace's comfort we decided it would be best to paddle to my truck, which we had shuttled to the end of Gargantua Road, and have Kerry drive her to the hospital in Wawa. In the meantime, John and I set up camp on the beach near the parking area and waited.

By 10 p.m. we were sitting on the beach still waiting. Sundown brought a sharp change in the weather. The temperature plummeted and we could hear a line of rain squalls approaching from the west. As we ducked for cover the wind fell off, though the rain began falling hard against the parched soil. John and I lay beside each other inside the tent, silently spending the time counting the seconds between flashes of lightning and the echoing thunder, and consciously keeping tabs on our bodies for the initial symptoms of food poisoning — headache, nausea, severe stomach cramps.

By morning the storm had gone and so had our worries about the highway diner's food. To celebrate, John and I pumped up the camp stove and cooked a stack of buttermilk pancakes, spiced with cinnamon.

Beachcombing at Warp Bay, Lake Superior.

An hour later, still working on my second helping of flapjacks, I saw Kerry and Grace wandering back up to the campsite. I quickly leapt to my feet, ran down the beach to meet them, and gasping for breath, asked, "Well, was it food poisoning?"

"Worse," Kerry replied. "Try a hernia an hour away from peritonitis settling in." We all just stood there dumbfounded.

So, choosing to recover from her operation on the sandy shores of Lake Superior rather than in a hotel room in Wawa, Grace stayed back at camp while we took turns daytripping up the coast. The first day we explored Gargantua Harbour itself, rummaging through the ruins of the once-thriving fishing village that dates back to 1871. The place is deserted now, with only two rustic shacks remaining. Just out from the deteriorated docks, the barely submerged skeletal remains of the 150-foot wooden tug *Columbus* can be seen. In 1909 the ship caught fire at the docks and was pulled out to the harbour and left to sink there.

On the island at the mouth of Gargantua Harbour lies yet another historical gem — the charred ruins of the Miron Lighthouse. The structure was built in 1889 and was tended by three generations of the Miron family. The light was dismantled in 1948, and now a solar-powered automatic beacon has taken its place upon the bleak rock.

On the second day, with Superior still surprisingly calm, John and I paddled up to the mouth of the Gargantua River. We spent the first part of the morning paddling upstream, following woodland caribou tracks along the beach and chatting with a group of Fish and Wildlife specialists who were working in the area. We were amazed to learn that they had heard stories of Grace's ordeal back at their home base in Wawa. We then travelled north to have lunch near the Devil's Chair (a sacred place believed by the Ojibwa to be where the Great Spirit Nanabozho rested after jumping over the lake). Then on our way back to the campsite, we took time out to visit Devil's Warehouse Island to search for the sites where ochre might have been mined. On the east side of the island we found an incredible dome-shaped cave, probably used hundreds of years ago as a shelter by shamans while visiting Devil's Warehouse to gather the red-coloured rock used to paint the pictographs at Agawa Rock.

ABOVE: *Rock sculpture, Rhyolite Cove.* BELOW: *The sand beach at the mouth of the Gargantua River is one of the most picturesque campsites on the entire Lake Superior shoreline.*

These islands were not originally named after the Devil. This place, revered by the Ojibwa as the altar inside their cathedral, was renamed by Christian missionaries who saw their own Satan in the Great Spirit of the Native peoples. Even the voyageurs named Gargantua Bay itself after seeing a similarity between the antics of Nanabozho and the hero in the satirical romance *Gargantua and Pantagruel*, written by Rabelais in 1552.

John and I returned late in the day to find that Grace and Kerry had taken the time to pack in fresh groceries, and for our last night's dinner on Superior we gorged ourselves on milk, vegetables and beer. Kerry even opened a can of oysters. Poor Grace, keeping to her strict diet, slurped her soup as we feasted. We finished our dessert of strawberries and cognac (Grace had applesauce), and feeling somewhat guilty about our gluttony, we treated our hernia victim by chauffeuring her by canoe to the north end of the harbour, where the Coastal Hiking Trail leads to a prominent lookout point.

John, Kerry and I helped Grace hobble up to the ridgetop, and from the slab of rock we watched as the sun set, illuminating this wild place with its reddish glow. We stood in awe of the expanse of it all, questioning how a landscape so beautiful could be mistaken by the black-robed Jesuits as a home for the Devil. To us, Gargantua Harbour had become a place of benediction.

We stood there on that ridge until the stars came out, not saying anything, but everyone was quite conscious that if we had chosen to venture down the remote Sand River rather than being lured out into the calm of Lake Superior, our canoe trip to Northern Ontario would have ended as a tragedy.

TIME:
4 to 5 days (3 days in good weather)

DIFFICULTY:
Canoeists must be experienced in paddling rough water and prepared to spend two days out of three being windbound.

PORTAGES:
None

FEE:
You must purchase a provincial park interior camping permit at the Agawa Bay or Old Woman Bay campground gatehouse before heading out on Lake Superior.

ALTERNATIVE ACCESS:
Depart from the parking area for the Orphan Lake Trail, located a short distance north of the Coldwater–June Creek access point on the west side of Highway 17.

ALTERNATIVE ROUTES:
The trip can be extended by continuing north along the Lake Superior coastline to Cape Gargantua, making camp at Indian Harbour, and then returning south to the parking area at Gargantua Harbour.

OUTFITTERS:
U-Paddle-It Ltd.
Box 374, Pinewood Drive
Wawa, Ontario
P0S 1K0
(705) 856-1493

FOR MORE INFORMATION:
Lake Superior Provincial Park
Box 267
Wawa, Ontario
P0S 1K0
(705) 856-2284

MAPS:
The Ministry of Natural Resources Lake Superior Provincial Park coastline map

TOPOGRAPHIC MAPS:
41 N/7, 41 N/11, 41 N/10

Canoe companions Doug and Mike lead the way up Algonquin's McIntosh Creek.

Bibliography

Aniskowicz, Theresa. "A Well-Travelled Road." *Nature Canada*, summer 1993.

Barnes, Michael. *Temagami*. Erin: Boston Mills Press, 1992.

Bennet, Doug and Tim Tiner. *Up North: A Guide to Ontario's Wilderness from Blackflies to the Northern Lights*. Reed Books Canada, 1993.

Beymer, Robert. *A Paddler's Guide to Quetico Provincial Park*. Minnesota: W.A. Fisher Company, 1985.

Bray, Matt, and Ashley Thompson. *Temagami: A Debate on Wilderness*. Toronto: Dundurn Press, 1990.

Campbell, William A. *The French and Pickerel Rivers, Their History and Their People*. Sudbury, Ont.: Journal Printing, 1986.

Consolidated Amethyst Communications Inc. *Along the Trail with Ralph Brice in Algonquin Park*. 1980.

Forsey, Helen. "The Great Divide." *Nature Canada*, winter 1994.

Friends of Algonquin. *Algonquin Provincial Park Canoe Route Map*. 1995.

Friends of Algonquin in cooperation with the Ministry of Natural Resources, 1994. *Barron Canyon Trail: History of the Canyon*.

Friends of Killarney. *Killarney Provincial Park Canoe Route Map*. 1995.

Friends of Quetico. *Fascinating Facts: A Compendium of Intriguing Facts, Anecdotes and Questions on the Cultural and Natural History of Quetico*. 1984.

———. *Lake Names of Quetico Provincial Park*. 1992.

———. *Pages from the Past: Voyageurs and Early Explorers*. 1992.

———. *Quetico Provincial Park Canoe Route Map*. 1995.

Geddes, Hilda. *The Canadian Mississippi River*. Burnstown, Ont.: General Store Publishing House, 1988.

Hall, Nany. "Temagami: The Battle to Protect 'Deep Water' Country." *Borealis*, summer 1990.

Hodgins, Bruce W., and Jamie Benidickson. *The Temagami Experience*. Toronto: University of Toronto Press, 1989.

Kates, Joanne. *Exploring Algonquin Park*. Vancouver/Toronto: Douglas & McIntyre, 1983.

Littlejohn, Bruce M. *Quetico–Superior Country: Wilderness Highway to Wilderness Recreation. Friends of Quetico Park*. Reprinted from *Canadian Geographical Journal*, August/September 1965.

Ministry of Culture, Tourism and Recreation. *Adventures in Canoeing, Kayaking, Whitewater Rafting*. 1994.

Ministry of Natural Resources. *Bon Echo Provincial Park, 1994 Programme*. 1994.

———. *Frontenac Provincial Park, 1994 Programme*. 1994.

———. *Madawaska River Provincial Park Management Plan*. 1987.

Ministry of Natural Resources, Chapleau District. *Missinaibi Provincial Park* pamphlet (1990).

———. *Missinaibi River Canoe Route* pamphlet (1995).

Ministry of Natural Resources, Parks and Recreational Areas Branch, in cooperation with McClelland & Stewart. *Canoe Routes of Ontario.* Toronto: 1981.

Ministry of Natural Resources, Parry Sound District. *Wolf and Pickerel River Canoe Route* pamphlet.

Ministry of Natural Resources, Sudbury District. *French River Canoe Route Map.* 1994.

Ministry of Natural Resources, Temagami District. *Canoeing in the Temagami Area* (map). Temagami, Ont.

Ministry of Natural Resources, Wawa District. *White River Canoe Route* pamphlet.

Mississippi Valley Conservation Authority. *Mississippi River Canoe Route* pamphlet.

The Oxen and the Axe. Collected and edited by the Pioneers. Madoc: Madoc Printing & Publishing, 1983.

Raffan, James. *Wild Waters: Canoeing Canada's Wilderness Rivers.* Toronto: Key Porter Books, 1986.

Raffan, James, and Bert Horwood. *Canexus: The Canoe in Canadian Culture.* Toronto: Betelgeuse Books & Queen's University, 1988.

Rayburn, Alan. "Who's to Blame For Mistaken Names?" *Canadian Geographic,* August 1993.

Reid, Ron, and Janet Grand. *Canoeing Ontario's Rivers.* Vancouver/Toronto: Douglas & McIntyre, 1985.

Reid, Ron. "Pictured Waters." *Seasons,* spring 1990.

Wilson, Hap. *Missinaibi: Journey to the Northern Sky.* With the Canadian Canoe Association, 1994.

———. *Rivers of the Upper Ottawa Valley.* With the Canadian Canoe Association, 1993.

———. *Temagami Canoe Routes.* Ontario Ministry of Natural Resources, 1977.